Beethoven: The First Biography

LUDWIG van **BEETHOFEN**

Geb: den 16. Dezember 1770 zu Bonn.

Gest: den 26. März 1827 zu Wien.

JOHANN ALOYS SCHLOSSER

Beethoven
The First Biography

[1827]

Edited with an Introduction and Notes by
BARRY COOPER

Translated from the German by
Reinhard G. Pauly

AMADEUS PRESS
Reinhard G. Pauly, General Editor.
Portland, Oregon

Grateful acknowledgment is hereby made to Macmillan Press Ltd. for permission to reproduce an excerpt from *The Letters of Beethoven* (London 1961), translated and edited by Emily Anderson, which appears on pages 158 and 159 of this edition.

Endpapers (Beethoven's letter to Abbé Stadler, 1826) courtesy Museum of Czech Literature, Prague; *frontispiece* (lithograph engraving by Josef Kriehuber, 1827) courtesy Historisches Museum der Stadt Wien.

Very special thanks to the Wahlquist Library, Ira F. Brilliant Center for Beethoven Studies, San José, California, for providing photographs of the original front cover, title page, dedication page, and back cover to Schlosser's book, reproduced on pages 21, 23, 25, and 160, respectively, of this edition.

Printed in Singapore

AMADEUS PRESS
The Haseltine Buildling
133 S.W. Second Avenue, Suite 450
Portland, Oregon 97204, U.S.A.

Library of Congress Cataloging-in-Publication Data

Schlosser, Johann Aloys.
      [Ludwig van Beethoven. English]
      Beethoven : the first biography, 1827 / Johann Aloys
Schlosser; edited with an introduction and notes by Barry
Cooper; translated from the German by Reinhard G. Pauly.
            p.   cm.
      Translation of: Ludwig van Beethoven.
      Includes bibliographical references (p.   ) and index.
      ISBN 1-57467-006-9
      1. Beethoven, Ludwig van, 1770-1827. 2. Composers—
Germany—Biography. I. Cooper, Barry (Barry A. R.) II. Title.
ML410.B4S3413   1996
780′.92—dc20
      [B]   95-36631

B
BEETHOVEN,
Ludwig VAN

Contents

Translator's Preface

My curiosity about the very first biographical study of Beethoven was aroused in conversations with Dr. William Meredith, director of the Ira F. Brilliant Center for Beethoven Studies in San José, California. The center's library owns a copy of Schlosser's rare book.

Dr. Meredith was kind enough to supply a photographic copy of the book, which I read with interest. Though Schlosser's account has some flaws, we agreed that an annotated English translation would be a valuable addition to the Beethoven literature.

That literature is vast. The fact that this is the very first attempt at a biography, written in the year of the composer's death, lends it significance, for it provides a contemporary view of Beethoven, the man and the musician. The introduction to this edition discusses the work's flaws as well as its merits.

During a month's stay in Vienna I was able to do some initial research. I then approached Dr. Barry Cooper, one of today's outstanding Beethoven scholars, and was delighted that he agreed to provide an introduction and editorial notes for this, the first modern edition in any language of Schlosser's 1827 study.

Reinhard G. Pauly

Introduction

Virtually nothing is known about the life of Johann Aloys Schlosser. François-Joseph Fétis reports that he was born in the small town of Lann, in Bohemia, around 1790; in 1827–28 he was a partner in the publishing firm of Buchler, Stephani & Schlosser in Prague, at which time he published brief biographies of both Mozart and Beethoven. Whether he knew Beethoven at all is by no means certain, and his biography gives no indication that he did. Beethoven had, however, visited Prague several times—notably when he performed there in 1796 and 1798, and also on his way from his home in Vienna to Teplitz in 1812—and his reputation in the Bohemian capital was quite considerable (see Pulkert 1988). The principal significance of Schlosser's biography is that it was the very first on Beethoven to be published, and that it appeared within a few months of the composer's death, some thirteen years before the next one.

Schlosser's book is dated 1828. It must have appeared earlier, however, for Anton Schindler wrote a letter dated 14 September

1827 to Ignaz Moscheles in which he said: "In Prague one Herr Schlosser has published a highly wretched biography of Beethoven" (see Brenneis 1979, 112). Schindler's information is corroborated by a notice by Jacob Hotschevar dated 20 September 1827 that clearly indicates the author's acquaintance with Schlosser's book (see Thayer, Deiters and Riemann eds. 1917–23, and note 61). Schlosser's preface is dated June 1827, but he refers to an event that took place on 27 July (see note 72). Thus his book must have appeared between this date and the date of Schindler's letter, and it probably came out in early September, with copies becoming available in Vienna for Schindler and Hotschevar almost immediately.

It is possible that there were two editions, and that the one seen by Schindler and Hotschevar was actually dated 1827. All known copies, however, are dated 1828, and although some lack either the frontispiece or the facsimile of Beethoven's letter to Abbé Maximilian Stadler, this is probably due to later damage rather than a difference in production. (The copy in the Nationalbibliothek in Vienna lacks the letter, while the one in the Beethoven Center in San José, California, lacks the frontispiece.) It seems, therefore, that only one edition was ever produced, and that it was postdated (a practice not uncommon even today).

So many books have been published on Beethoven since Schlosser's that it is difficult to imagine a time when there were none. At that time, anyone who wanted a rounded picture of Beethoven's life would have had to collate information from Ernst Ludwig Gerber's lexicon of 1790–92 and 1812–14, which gives a brief account of Beethoven's life up to 1810 (facsimile in Gerber, Wessely ed. 1966–77), with other information taken from various newspapers and music journals, together with personal reminiscences by any acquaintances that could be found. This was, as Schlosser says, "a task requiring no small effort," especially for anyone who did not live in Vienna. Thus Schlosser's brief biography satisfied an immediate need, whereas a full-scale biography could not have been produced for some years. Indeed, the next significant milestone in Beethoven biography was not until 1838, when the composer's friends Franz Wegeler and Ferdinand Ries published a loose but important collection of biographical reminiscences, as *Biographische Notizen über Ludwig van Beethoven* (see Wegeler and Ries 1987). This was followed in 1840 by a longer but very inaccurate biography by Schindler, but it was not until the work of Alexander Wheelock Thayer toward the end of the nineteenth century that a full and fairly reliable biography was prepared.

It is uncertain what sources Schlosser used. He clearly consulted Gerber's lexicon, since his accounts of Bach and Handel derive from there, but little of his material concerning Beethoven himself is closely related to Gerber's. Some of it is probably based on interviews with Beethoven's acquaintances, including the book's dedicatee Conradin Kreutzer, and Abbé Stadler, from whom Schlosser obtained and reproduced a copy of the aforementioned letter. Other parts may have come from newspaper reports around the time of Beethoven's death. Schlosser may even have been present himself at Beethoven's funeral and the subsequent memorial services in Vienna. His preface indicates that he was in Vienna in June 1827, and he was no doubt collecting information at that time. It seems very probable, too, that he attended the memorial service in Prague that he describes. His attempts to gather material do not appear to have been very systematic, however, and this is reflected in the rather piece-meal content and structure of the book.

The book is far from wholly reliable, as many writers have pointed out. Schindler's bad opinion of it has already been mentioned; Hotschevar described it as "filled with many essential inaccuracies" and gave details about one of them (see note 61). Both these writers, however, had ulterior motives for condemning the book. Schindler was making plans to write his own version of Beethoven's biography and was perhaps also annoyed to see a biography that included no mention of himself. Meanwhile Hotschevar had allied himself with a rival enterprise, led by Anton Gräffer, to produce an official biography of Beethoven—a plan that never came to fruition. Thus both Hotschevar and Schindler would have had a vested interest in trying to limit sales of Schlosser's book by heaping scorn upon it, and their influential position has no doubt colored the views of many others.

Already in 1828 there was published a dismissive review by Friedrich Deyks in Schott's music journal *Caecilia* (8:129–131; see Pečman 1978, 349), and several later writers have been equally critical. Thayer pointed out the two major errors in Schlosser's first two sentences and left his readers to judge the worth of the rest by inference (Thayer, Forbes ed. 1967, 64), while Maynard Solomon (1977, x) has dismissed the book as a "worthless and error-filled biography." Several other writers, some of whom one suspects have never actually read the book, have been equally scathing.

These criticisms are not wholly invalid, though they are at times overstated. The book does contain factual errors, as well as some questionable statements for which there is no corroborative evidence (several of the statements about Beethoven's childhood come in this category). Much of the remainder merely reproduces information that is now readily available from other sources, and it includes some lengthy digressions. There are huge omissions, such as Beethoven's concert tour of 1796, his dealings with publishers such as Muzio Clementi and Anton Steiner, his legal struggle for the guardianship of his nephew, his religious outlook, and his literary interests. The judgments of Beethoven's music toward the end of the book are very meager and totally ignore his more recent compositions, apart from a few general remarks about them being thoroughly unified but difficult to comprehend (which is true enough but hardly suffices, even for a short book). Thus one should not turn to Schlosser for a balanced and accurate picture of Beethoven's life, and Oldřich Pulkert (1988, 431) has rightly described the author as "more an enthusiast than a biographer."

Nevertheless, the book does have its value, especially as a reflection of what was generally known and believed about Beethoven at the time of his death, and Schlosser's detailed account of the events immediately after his death—events that were still fresh in the author's mind—is particularly illuminating. Useful too are his amusing anecdotes, probably not recorded elsewhere, of Beethoven's habit of making cryptic remarks such as "Da capo!" or "So, from Bremen!", which would delight or mystify his listeners depending on whether or not the reference was understood. They confirm one's impression that Beethoven had a quick and ready wit—a characteristic that is perhaps also discernible in some of his music.

Not all early comments on the book were hostile either. Joseph Fröhlich (1780–1862), in an article on Beethoven's Ninth Symphony in *Caecilia* in 1828 (8:231–256), applauded

Schlosser's suggestion that the Fifth Symphony signals the beginning of Beethoven's third period. And an anonymous essay in the *Foreign Quarterly Review* of 1831 (8:439–461) used Schlosser as a starting point for a general discussion of musical genius and talent.

The number of surviving copies of the book—nearly a dozen are known in the United States alone—also suggests it was a greater commercial success than has hitherto been supposed. Moreover, its outright errors are not nearly as numerous as one might be led to believe by some writers, and most are errors of detail. For example, Schlosser states that, as a result of Jerome Bonaparte's invitation to Beethoven to leave Vienna, three Viennese noblemen whom he names agreed in 1809 to pay Beethoven 2000 gulden a year to remain. All this is perfectly accurate except that the sum was 4000 gulden per annum; but even here Schlosser is not as misleading as might appear, since inflation reduced the value of the annuity to something closer to 2000 gulden. Schlosser is also helpful in dispelling a myth about Beethoven and a spider, which had been circulated quite widely (Schlosser points out that the story applies to a different composer with a fairly similar name).

Often his portrait of Beethoven is quite accurate. His claim that in the 1800s Beethoven's fame as a composer was such that "music dealers vied with each other," and that the composer was no longer obliged to give lessons but often did so as a favor without asking for payment, is corroborated by other evidence. So too is his picture of Beethoven doing most of his composing outdoors, noting his ideas on paper then and there, and writing out the scores later in his room. Schlosser also correctly records that Beethoven spent large sums of money on his nephew and had a strong sense of family relationships generally. (What Schlosser omits, however, is the heated arguments and hostility that sometimes resulted from such strong emotional attachments.) His portrayal of Beethoven's character in general is also perceptive and is broadly in line with other people's observations. Many of these details, such as Beethoven's tendency to become so absorbed in composing that he would miss meals, would not have been widely known at the time, and so Schlosser's account, for all its faults, would have provided a useful introduction for those who knew Beethoven only through his music.

Most significantly, in contrast to Schindler, Schlosser seems to have made no attempt to distort or fabricate evidence. Nearly all Beethoven biographies have suffered to a greater or lesser extent from following Schindler's inaccuracies and deliberate falsifications, some of which are still coming to light. Here we have one of the very few accounts that is wholly free from Schindlerian influence—both invented "facts" and misleading opinions (Schindler may even have refused to cooperate). The biographical reminiscences of Wegeler and Ries are another such book, but even the reminiscences of Gerhard von Breuning, who also knew Beethoven, contain several passages that derive ultimately from Schindler's imagination (see Breuning, Solomon ed. 1992).

Partly as a result of its poor press reports, Schlosser's book has never been reprinted in German; it has also never been available in English, and even English extracts from it are rare. The purpose of the present edition is not to provide a clear and vivid picture of Beethoven's life, for which one must turn to more reliable and better balanced accounts (see, for example, Thayer, Forbes ed. 1967 and Solomon 1977), but to enable English-speaking readers to judge Schlosser's book for themselves rather than relying on secondhand criticisms, and also to illuminate what was known and believed in Vienna and Prague in 1827—not only about Beethoven but about his relationship to Haydn and Mozart, and to the music of Bach and Handel. (It is interesting to note how prominently the latter two figure in the book, while their contemporaries Telemann and Fux, equally renowned in their day, had already been forgotten.)

Schlosser's factual errors have been corrected in the editorial notes. This does not mean, however, that the remainder is necessarily true: in some cases there is insufficient evidence to know, while elsewhere one or two errors of detail could well have been overlooked. The editorial notes are also used to amplify, clarify, or modify Schlosser's account, so that a fuller picture emerges. Brief editorial interventions have been indicated within the text in square brackets, while longer comments are to be found at the back of the book. Schlosser himself provided several footnotes—some of them very lengthy digressions; as in the original, these have been retained as footnotes to the main text. For most purposes they can be ignored, since they throw little light on Beethoven, but they provide further illustrations of the interests and concerns of his contemporaries at the time of his death.

I am most grateful to Reinhard Pauly for suggesting this project to me, and for providing me with photocopies of the book and the notes he made on the subject in Vienna, as well as for his translation, to which I have made minor editorial amendments here and there.

Barry Cooper
University of Manchester

Ludwig van Beethoven's

BIOGRAPHIE

herausgegeben

von

J. A. Schlosser.

Ludwig van Beethoven.

A

Biography

together with assessments of his works.

Published

with the aim of erecting a monument to his teacher,

Joseph Haydn,[1]

by

Joh. Aloys Schlosser.

With a lithograph facsimile of one of Beethoven's letters.

Prague:

by Buchler, Stephani and Schlosser.

1828.

Ludwig van Beethoven.

Eine

Biographie

desselben, verbunden mit Urtheilen über seine Werke.

Herausgegeben

zur Erwirkung eines Monuments für dessen Lehrer,

Joseph Haydn,

von

Joh. Aloys Schlosser.

Mit einem lythographirten Briefe Beethoven's.

Prag:

bei Buchler, Stephani und Schlosser.

1828.

To my

highly honored friend,

the

Kapellmeister to Prince Fürstenberg,

Herrn

Conradin Kreutzer.[2]

No memorial is needed
for the master of immortal sound,
whose never-fading song
is honored in this work;
the thankfulness that my heart so willingly offers
is itself testament enough;
for the magic of his art
has been felt by us all,
so for these blissful hours
may he be honored, praised, and thanked! —
You, noble sir,
who have made great strides
on the road to fame,
consider — if it please you —
this work as an offering of my love
and esteem for you![3]

J. A. Schlosser.

An meinen

hochverehrten Freund,

den

fürstlich fürstenbergischen Kapellmeister,

Herrn

Conradin Kreutzer.

Bedarf es gleich des Denkmahls nicht,
Das ich dem Meister hoher Klänge,
Der nie verhallenden Gesänge,
Durch dieses Werk geweiht; so spricht
Doch laut sich aus die Dankbarkeit,
Die ihm mein Herz so willig beut;
Denn was dem Zauber seiner Kunst gelang,
Hat Jeder, so wie ich, empfunden,
D'rum für die wonnevollen Stunden
Sey ihm gebracht Lob, Preis und Dank! —
Dich, edler Mann,
Der auf des Ruhmes Bahn
So glänzend vorgeschritten,
Mög' es, — darum will ich Dich bitten —
Als Opfer meiner Liebe ehren,
Und meine Achtung Dir bewähren!

J. A. Schlosser.

Preface

Beethoven's death has been noted with more grief, in Germany and throughout Europe, than anyone else's for a long time. His art reached a level far above what others will attain. We therefore grieve not only because of our loss but also because there is no one able to take his place. Beethoven was not only a great artist but also a great human being; there is therefore general desire for a biography.

I have undertaken to put one together, a task requiring no small effort. In presenting my work to the grieving public, I aim to satisfy this wish but also to accomplish another purpose. Beethoven's death in Vienna was observed with solemn rites. At that time measures were taken to honor his memory by an appropriate monument.[4] Although efforts have been underway for a long time to raise funds for the construction of similar monuments for Haydn and Mozart, these aims have so far not been accomplished. Some claim that there is no need — that both men, in their compositions, have created the best possible monuments to their own honor. But monuments we create for the dead chiefly honor us, as expressions of our gratitude. Indeed, we would rightly be blamed by posterity if our appreciation were not to find some lasting, tangible expression.

I intend to publish a life of Mozart,[5] hoping that with the proceeds a monument for him can be built. But before that I trust that this biography of Beethoven may make it possible to honor Haydn in the same manner. Who honors Beethoven must also honor Haydn, his teacher, for only

through Haydn did Beethoven become what he is for us. Using the proceeds from this book for a Haydn
monument means that those who buy
it will be doubly rewarded.

This is the best way to further my
goal, and I have no doubt that others
will gladly help me. We must not let
ourselves be put to shame by the stones
that, according to the ancient fable,
formed themselves into monuments,
to honor the masters of harmony.[6]

Those who, by a special contribu-
tion, wish to make possible a more
magnificent structure than could be
built with the funds generated by the

sale of this book alone should indicate this as soon as possible. For the time being, a written pledge will do. Later I shall give more detailed information about how these funds will be put to use; actual contributions will be accepted then. The names of these special contributors will be preserved for posterity in [= on?] the monument.

I cannot expect every reader to be familiar with the artists I mention, nor to have easy access to Gerber's lexicon.[7] I have therefore provided notes to help. They do not, however, offer information about Haydn and Mozart. My biography of the latter serves that purpose, and I intend soon to publish a detailed biography of the former as well.[8]

If Beethoven's biography does not contain as many interesting details as those of Haydn and Mozart, this is not my fault. Rather it is due to the relatively few contacts he had with others and to the little travel he undertook. Also he produced less than those two, although he had as much will and as much suffering.

The portrait of the dear departed that I include is the best among all that have been created. It is one of Kriehuber's masterworks, based on the better of the two busts by Anton Dietrich, the famous sculptor for whom Beethoven sat.[9]

A letter by the deceased is included in a lithographic reproduction. For this I am indebted to his friend the esteemed Abbé Stadler.[10] Beethoven wrote this letter to Stadler, who had sent him a copy of Stadler's publication defending the authenticity of Mozart's Requiem.[11] Readers will find this reproduction of interest because it shows the composer's handwriting, including musical notation. It reveals some aspects of his personality better than I could. At the same time the letter demonstrates his high regard for Mozart and Stadler, and also his opinion of Weber.[12] The reproduction is very true to the original. Herr Stadler and I found a few words impossible to read. Rather than indulging in guesswork I leave it to the reader to decipher them.

For now I shall not invite any artists to submit ideas for the monument. This will have to wait until I can determine the amount of money available for that purpose.

Vienna, June 1827.
The Author.

Weil er der Selige ist, so kannst du der Glück-
liche seyn.

SCHILLER.[13]

He is blessed, and you are therefore fortunate.

Ludwig van Beethoven was born in Bonn in 1772.[14] His father, Anton van Beethoven,[*] was a tenor in the chapel of Maximilian Friedrich, the Elector of Cologne.[15]

---

[*]In the Netherlands we find many non-aristocratic families who use *van* in their name, just as there are many in France who use *de*. This applies to the Beethovens, a middle-class family. Their name derives from their ancestors' residence, a *Mayerhof* [beet farm]. On the other hand, several German families do not use *von* though their nobility goes back farther than that of others who do include *von* in their name. This is true of the Dalbergs (formerly Talburg), who can trace

Ludwig's talent for music manifested itself in his early youth. In this
he resembles most of our greatest composers. Before he was four years old he
greatly enjoyed listening while his father, seated at the keyboard, prepared
himself for a performance. Ludwig
then would happily leave his playmates

---

their line to Cajo Marcello; of the Böckel or
Begel family, equally ancient, and of the
Volkhart family (formerly Volkert, as their
estate in Neukurhessen is still called), who
trace their lineage to Count Volkert in the
Nibelungen Lied, that is, farther back than
the time of Charlemagne. It is also true of
the Heissenstamm or Heissenstein house, of
the Mühlhausen, formerly Muhlhusen; the
Münche, formerly Monke; the Bose, formerly Buse; and so on.

Beethoven's birthhouse, by Beissel, 1889.
Courtesy Beethoven-Haus, Bonn.

to listen; if his father seemed about to stop, the boy would urge him to continue. But his greatest pleasure was to sit on his father's lap and with his little fingers accompany him in a song. It was not long before Ludwig would repeat this little game by himself. When he was barely in his fifth year he did this so well that serious music lessons seemed called for. At first the father provided these, and the boy progressed so rapidly that a more thorough teacher was required.

The best keyboard player in Bonn was van der Eden, the court organist.[16] Ludwig's father could not afford him as a teacher for his son, but van der Eden offered to teach the boy free of charge. Being both organist and a member of the Elector's court chapel, he was very busy; moreover he needed to earn additional income by giving lessons. This left little time for Ludwig's instruction, but in spite of this the boy made such remarkable progress that he became known in Bonn as a child prodigy.

Father and teacher were eager to bring the boy's talent to the Elector's attention. Having heard the young musician but once, the ruler was so impressed that he ordered van der

Eden to instruct the boy daily at the prince's expense. For Ludwig this was the greatest possible incentive. He soon progressed to the point where he often played in the chapel and also in the Elector's private chamber.

An anecdote has often been told which was meant to show that Beethoven's extraordinary sensitivity, later on so characteristic of him, already existed during his childhood. The story first appeared in the Leipziger musikalische Zeitung (vol. 2, no. 57)[17] and was repeated in several other journals. I relate it here only to prevent its continued attribution to Beethoven.

According to the Leipzig journal:

A boy was intended by his parents to become an outstanding musician. By the time he was eight years old his violin playing amazed everyone. He was forced to practice at least three-fourths of every day, confined like a prisoner to a small room. His only companion there was a huge spider. As soon as the boy started practicing, the spider would leave its web in the corner and, attracted by the extraordinarily beautiful sounds, would approach the boy. Soon they became such good friends that the spider would first descend to the music stand, then from the stand to the boy, and finally would rest on his bow arm. In his solitude, the spider provided companionship; when the boy left the room, he was soon anxious to return to his friend. Perhaps his musical progress, which was already widely admired, was largely due to his spider!

One day his aunt, who cared for him as a mother, entered the room with someone who had come to admire his talent. After the first few notes the spider appeared as usual, came closer and closer, and rested on the young artist's hand. Alas! All at once the aunt took off one of her slippers, quickly cast the ugly spider from its favorite place to the floor — and stepped on it. The poor child did not cry out, nor did he weep: he fell to the floor unconscious. He was taken to his bed, where he remained senseless. For more than three months he remained on the brink of death, and when he finally regained his power of speech, his first wish was to see his beloved spider.

The young artist is the now famous Beethoven. Those who doubt the truth of this account may have it verified by his teacher at that time, citizen Le Mierra in Paris.

Doctor Hagen in Altenburg.

Dr. Hagen had read this anecdote in Disjouval's *Arachnologie*, but he confused the names Beethoven and Berthaume.[*][18] Disjouval begins his account with these words: "The famous

---

[*]Before the French Revolution Berthaume was the owner and director of the Paris Concerts Spirituels. In 1791 he went to Germany where he concertized extensively. From 1793 to 1801 he was concertmaster for the Duke of Oldenburg and the prince bishop of Lübeck in Eutin. He then accepted a position as first violinist in St. Petersburg but died there, still in 1801. He always confirmed the truth of the spider anecdote.

Berthaume, one of the foremost violin virtuosos, while still a boy, was intended by his parents," and so forth. Beethoven never had a teacher named Le Mierra.

When van der Eden died in 1782, Christian Gottlob Neefe[*] (who had

---

[*]Christian Gottlob Neefe was born on 5 February 1748 in Chemnitz, Saxony. While a law student in Leipzig he studied music with Hiller.[19] In 1776 he succeeded Hiller as music director for Seyler's troupe of actors near Dresden; he traveled with this company to Frankfurt am Main, Mainz, Cologne, Hanau, Mannheim, and Heidelberg. In Frankfurt [in 1778] he married the singer [Susanne] Zink, who had been trained by [Georg] Benda. Formerly in the employ of the ducal court at Gotha, she had

previously been designated to succeed him) became court organist.

The Elector instructed Neefe to consider young Beethoven's musical education one of his most important

---

joined the Seyler company as actress and singer. That troupe disbanded, and in 1779 Neefe and his wife joined the theater company of Grossmann and Helmuth in Bonn. There the Elector Maximilian Friedrich appointed him court organist in 1782. Both Neefes were also employed in the Elector's theater. After the Elector's death in 1784, his successor[20] continued their appointments. During the French occupation their salaries were no longer paid. In 1796 Neefe and his family went to Leipzig and then to Dessau, where he died on 26 January 1798. He left three daughters and a son who, in Vienna, became one of our most distinguished painters of theater scenery.

Christian Gottlob Neefe (1748–1798),
copper engraving by Gottlob Liebe after
Johann Georg Rosenberg. Courtesy
Gesellschaft der Musikfreunde, Vienna.

assignments.[21] This pleased Neefe, who had already noted the talents of his future pupil. He was glad to do everything possible for him, especially since Ludwig was very fond of him and tried to please him by showing great industry.

After Maximilian Friedrich's death his successor, an Austrian prince, showed continued interest in the boy. He set aside an even larger sum for his instruction and also favored teacher and pupil in various ways.

Neefe's compositions do not display the force or brilliance of a great genius; they did not give rise to an artistic revolution or a change in taste. But they are unmistakably the products of talent, skill, sensitivity, and good taste. They speak to his abilities as a very good teacher of a young artist — probably a better teacher than a person of great genius would be. Moreover, his character was marked by honesty and sincerity; he was accommodating, open, and friendly, which traits were bound to have a good influence on the young Beethoven.

Neefe lost no time introducing his pupil to music of the highest quality and taste: the works of Johann Sebastian Bach.[*] Neefe pointed out to his

---

[*]Johann Sebastian Bach, court composer to the King of Poland, Kapellmeister to the Duke of Weissenfels and the Prince of Anhalt-Cöthen, music director at the St. Thomas School in Leipzig. He was born on 21 March 1685 in Eisenach, where his father Johann Ambrosius Bach was a musician employed by the court and state. Before he was ten years old he lost his parents and was taken in by his older brother Johann Christoph, organist in Oedruff [Ohrdruf], under whose guidance he learned the rudiments of keyboard playing. By then he was already so strongly attracted to music that he secretly took from his brother a book with keyboard compositions by Froberger, Kerll, and Pachelbel, which his brother would not lend him, and copied the entire book at night by moonlight within six weeks. He then furtively played it, until his brother

found out and took away both the book and the copy, wanting to teach the boy first the necessary prerequisites. He was also concerned that too much time spent at the keyboard would interfere with the required school work. After his brother's death, Sebastian attended the Lüneburg Gymnasium [high school]. From there he often undertook the arduous [foot] journey to Thamburg [Hamburg], to hear the famous organist Johann Adam Reinken. He also journeyed to Celle to listen to the ducal musicians, most of whom were French, as he wanted to become familiar with the style of French music.

In 1703 he became a court musician in Weimar, and in 1704, organist in Arnstadt. There he acquired most of the musical education that would later enable him to become a great composer and organist. He accomplished this partly by studying the works of Bruhns, Reinken, and Buxtehude, partly by his own reflecting and practicing. In 1706 he spent three months in Lübeck, anx-

ious to learn all he could from Dietrich Buxtehude, the famous organist.

He left Arnstadt in 1707 to become organist in Mühlhausen, but a year later he accepted the post of court organist in Weimar.
It was a distinguished position, and his
organ playing flourished. He wrote more
works for the church in Weimar than any-
where else. In 1714 he was also appointed
concertmaster but was still expected to
compose and perform all the necessary
works for the church.

In 1717 Bach emerged as the victor in a
French attack on German art. In that year
Jean Louis Marchand, banned from Paris,
appeared in Dresden. Marchand, born in
Lyon in 1669, had been the royal organist
in Versailles; he had also served at several
Paris churches. He had the reputation of
being the world's foremost player of the
organ and harpsichord. In Paris, anyone
with musical aspirations insisted on studying with him for at least a month. A lesson
with him cost one Louis d'or, and he rented

twenty lodgings so that he could teach in every neighborhood in the city. His fame in Dresden caused the King of Poland to offer him the post of organist with a salary of 3500 thaler.

At this time Volumier was concertmaster at the Dresden court. From other Frenchmen, or from his own experience, he had learned that Marchand was an intriguer. He wished to humiliate him or, better yet, see him removed from his court position. He therefore wrote to Bach, asking him to come to Dresden at once to engage in a contest with the Frenchman who derided German art. Bach came. With the king's approbation, and without Marchand's knowledge, Bach was admitted to the next concert at court. Marchand performed variations on a little French song. His variations were artful, his execution was pleasant and full of fire, and he was applauded. Bach, who was standing next to him, was then asked to play. He sat down at the keyboard and improvised a short but masterful prelude that led into the song Marchand had just performed. Bach's twelve variations on it were far more beautiful and artistic, bringing far greater applause, much to Marchand's embarrassment. But Bach did not let it go at that: he presented the proud Frenchman with a small piece of paper on which he had pencilled a theme. He invited him to a friendly organ contest, asking Marchand in turn to give him a theme. From what he had heard so far, Marchand was already convinced of his opponent's superior skills. He promised to give Bach such a theme and to enter such a contest, but he quickly departed from Dresden before the appointed day, so that Bach alone entertained the invited guests with his supreme artistry.

Upon his return to Weimar he received an offer from the Prince of Anhalt-Cöthen to become his Kapellmeister, which he accepted the same year.

In 1723 the Leipzig town council offered Bach an even more favorable position: to become director of music at the famous St.

Thomas School. Shortly after this the Duke of Weissenfels bestowed on him the Kapellmeister title. On several occasions Bach presented himself to the Dresden court, performing on the organ; as a result, in 1736, the king appointed him court composer. He journeyed to Berlin in 1747 and was invited to play for the [Prussian] king in Potsdam. The king gave him a theme on which to improvise a fugue. Bach acquitted himself very well, whereupon the king requested of him a six-part fugue. Bach did this extremely well, too, this time on a theme of his own choosing. On his return to Leipzig, he further composed two ricercars, in three and six voices, on the royal theme. These he had engraved [in the *Musical Offering*, BWV 1079], and he dedicated them to the king.

He underwent eye surgery, which was unsuccessful. As a result, his previously excellent health declined, and he died of a stroke on 28 July 1750.[22]

One of Bach's successors at the St. Thomas School was the famous Hiller, who, in his *Lebensbeschreibungen berühmter Musik-gelehrten*, on page 25, said of Bach:

"If ever a composer excelled in full poly-phonic writing, it was Johann Sebastian Bach. If ever a musical artist explored the most hidden secrets of harmony and put them to the highest artistic use, it surely was the same Bach. Such works of art, when constructed by others, may seem dry, but he, more than anyone else, imbued them with fresh invention. No sooner had he heard a musical theme than he imagined all the artful ways in which it might be treated. His melodies were always unusual, original, inventive, and unlike those of any other composer. His serious disposition tended to draw him to music that was well con-structed, serious, and profound, but where it seemed appropriate he was also capable of a lighter, bantering manner, especially in his playing. He was so versed in composing pieces in many voices that he could read, at a glance, all simultaneously sounding parts in a large score. His hearing was so keen that

pupil their intrinsic value and helped him cope with the great difficulties of execution involved in their perform-

---

he could detect the slightest mistake even in the most complex composition. When he conducted, he insisted on precise execution, and he never failed to choose and maintain the right tempo, usually a very lively one.

"There is no doubt that he was the best keyboard player of his day, and perhaps also of days yet to come. Proof of this can be found in his keyboard compositions: everyone who knows them finds them difficult, yet he performed them with ease, as though they were mere musettes. In playing he used all fingers equally, resulting in renditions of the greatest dexterity. With ingenious fingerings of his own invention, he executed the most difficult passages with supreme fluency and ease. The use of the thumbs contributed to this. Up to then even the most famous players seldom if ever used them."

ance. In this way Beethoven, even in his early years, received the best possible guidance. Once a person's mind has been opened to that which is noble and great, he will no longer be attracted to the low and ignoble. By playing Bach's music, the boy developed the dexterity that distinguished his playing in later years. Before he had reached the age of eleven he had played Bach's *Well-Tempered Clavier*, which consists of twice twenty-four preludes and fugues in all keys.[23] Even advanced players find it difficult to perform these magnificent preludes and fugues properly; it is all the more remarkable that a boy of that age would perform them to the general applause of artists.

Beethoven began composing in his ninth year.[24] Since van der Eden gave him no instruction in this, the boy's efforts did not conform to rules. Yet knowledgeable people predicted that with instruction there would soon be better results. After Neefe began teaching the boy, these predictions were fulfilled immediately, and in his eleventh year Beethoven wrote nine variations on a march theme, three keyboard sonatas, and several songs. These were engraved and published in

Speyer and Mannheim.[25] Though the attempts of a beginner, these works did honor to their young composer.

Early in life Ludwig showed decided talent for varying and developing a theme in improvisation. An account of Beethoven astounding an audience in 1790 by such an improvisation on a theme by a certain Pastor Junker was related by the latter (himself a capable pianist and composer, who died in 1797 in Rupertshofen near Kirchberg) in an autobiographical sketch in part three of the *Würtembergisches Repertorium der Literatur.*[26]

Beethoven's dexterous and expressive playing also was admired at this early stage. In both skills he soon outdid his teacher. He excelled at both piano and organ playing. As a result, the Elector designated him to become Neefe's successor and as early as 1791 conferred on him the title of court organist.[27]

Anxious to have Beethoven receive more advanced training than his local teacher could provide, the Elector in 1792 sent him to Vienna, paying all expenses, so that Ludwig could perfect his compositional skills under the great Haydn's tutelage. This instruction had the desired results. Haydn was happy with his task and became fond of his young pupil. Ludwig, in turn, clung to him like a child to his father.

Beethoven was now made much better acquainted with Bach than he had been through Neefe. Only now did he arrive at a full understanding of Bach's music. Haydn then turned to the music of Handel,* eager to have his

---

*George Frideric Handel was born in Halle, in Magdeburg province, on 24 [23] February 1685. From his seventh to fourteenth year he was taught the foundations of organ playing and composing by the local organist [Friedrich Wilhelm] Zachau. In 1703 Handel went to Hamburg, where he presented *Almira*, his first opera, in 1704; by 1708 three more operas had followed. During these years he also taught clavier playing and published many keyboard pieces, songs, and cantatas. He then went to Florence, where he premiered his opera *Rodrigo*, and to Venice, where his *Agrippina* was given on twenty-seven consecutive nights. He continued on to Rome, where his serenata *Il trionfo del tempo* was heard, and to Naples for performances of his *Acis and Galatea* [*Aci, Galatea, e Polifemo*].

Leaving Italy in 1710 he journeyed to Hanover where the Elector made him his Kapellmeister, succeeding the venerable Steffani. With the Elector's approval he set out on another journey at the end of the year; it took him to England for the first time. There he completed *Rinaldo* within two weeks; it remained a favorite opera of the English for a long time.

After a year Handel returned to Hanover, but at the end of 1712 he was again granted permission to go to England. This time he became involved in so many activities there that he forgot all about Hanover.

Handel's prince acceded to the English throne in 1714. While still in Hanover he had been displeased by Handel's long absence, but as King George I he was soon mollified, both by Handel's accomplishments and by the intercession of the composer's patrons. Handel regained the new king's favor and was awarded a yearly salary of 400 pounds. From then on he composed for the stage and for concert performances. As an organist he was considered to be the greatest virtuoso of all.

Blindness afflicted him in his last year[s], but his energy did not leave him. He continued to play his organ works in public and was able to go on composing by dictating his ideas to a Mr. [John Christopher] Smith. Only six days before his death (he died on 13 [14] April 1759) he supervised the performance of one of his oratorios.

Handel's estate amounted to 20,000 pounds, 1000 of which he had willed to a foundling home in London; 19,000 pounds went to his relatives in Germany. A magnifi-

pupil also come to know that great contemporary of Bach.[28]

Haydn himself had taken these two as his models. Since he wanted Beethoven to study his own style, Haydn thought it best first to introduce him to Bach and Handel. That way Beethoven would easily recognize in which ways Haydn had gone beyond them.

As well as introducing his own works to his pupil, Haydn also acquainted him with those of Mozart,

---

cent marble monument of him was erected in London's Westminster Abbey; it takes up an entire arch of that church.29

who had died the year before Beethoven arrived in Vienna.[30] Thus exposed
to the greatest music ever written, Beethoven was bound to have his taste developed in the best possible way.

In 1795, however, the lessons were
interrupted since Haydn had agreed to
travel to London for the second time.[31]
He turned his pupil over to the care of
his friend Albrechtsberger,[*] a master
of contrapuntal writing.

---

[*]Johann Georg Albrechtsberger was born in
Klosterneuburg on 3 February 1736. Before
he was seven he became a choirboy in the
abbey there. Later he entered the school at
Melk Abbey where the organist Mann [=
Matthias Georg Monn] instructed him in

Albrechtsberger, like Haydn, de-
voted much love and care to Beethoven's instruction, and the pupil showed
his gratitude through great industry.[33]

---

the rudiments of thorough bass and composition. Albrechtsberger himself then became
organist at Melk and later in Raab. In 1772
he was appointed court organist in Vienna
and also choirmaster at the Carmelite mon-
astery there. By 1792 he had advanced to the
position of Kapellmeister at Vienna's cathe-
dral of St. Stephen; in 1799 he became an
honorary member of the Royal Swedish
Academy of Music. He died in Vienna on 24
May [7 March] 1809. Haydn contributed to
his fame by stating that of all the Viennese
masters Albrechtsberger was the best
teacher of composition. He was a very serious, upright human being, and a very good
husband and father. His music is simple but
great, and frequently noble and exalted.[32]

Johann Georg Albrechtsberger, engraving
by Johann Joseph Neidl after Gandolf
Stainhauser de Treuberg. Courtesy
Gesellschaft der Musikfreunde, Vienna.

While still in his native Germany, Beethoven had already acquired a basic command of Latin, Italian, and French. He now perfected his knowledge of these languages and also studied English.[34] History was another subject he pursued; it had attracted him in his youth and continued to occupy him until his death. He had a good memory for concepts and facts.

On Haydn's return Beethoven continued his studies with him and Albrechtsberger, writing several works that did credit to his instructors.[35] But he attracted even greater attention with his playing, which had already been excellent during his Bonn years. In Vienna he mastered enormously difficult music and increased his velocity. Free improvisation was his special skill, and his ability to vary a theme approached that of Mozart.

Beethoven's generous patron, the Elector, died in Vienna in 1801. His memory should ever be honored. Anyone who provides for the mundane, material needs of an artist, thus enabling him to bestow divine bliss on us, is entitled to posterity's gratitude. As we remember the artist, so should we also remember his benefactor.[36]

The Elector's death meant that

Beethoven could no longer expect a secure position in Bonn. Beethoven regretted this, for he had an attachment to his native city and even more to his family.[37] Yet he need not have worried about the loss of security. By this time he had become so well trained that he could be confident about finding other appointments. For the time being he could manage by himself. He had established such a fine reputation as a composer that music dealers vied with each other to obtain one of his scores; he could therefore sell them at a good price. This meant that he was not obliged to give lessons, though he acceded to requests for them in several instances. He generally did this as a favor, without asking for payment. All those whom he instructed were eternally grateful to him, and in most cases their achievements do him great honor.

Soon after the Elector's death an important noble Viennese family invited Beethoven to become their guest, thus intending to make up for his loss of support from other sources.[38] This meant that he could now live for his art alone, without any material worries. But it is rare to find in one human being these three talents combined:

art, genius, and wisdom in the practical affairs of everyday life. Beethoven was no such rare individual, and it was only natural that these living arrangements did not last, for such a situation requires mutual accommodation and agreement.

Critics have often been severe with Beethoven regarding these and similar matters, but one must excuse souls who are most sensitive to beauty. It is not realistic for us to expect those who dwell in the highest realms of art (and who are thereby capable of bringing artistic pleasures down to us ordinary mortals) to be always gracious, considerate, and attentive, or to display the feelings and moods experienced by the rest of us. The man of genius may move in celestial spheres and seek to transport us there with his creations, yet at the same time he may cause problems for us earthbound creatures. So many of us manage ordinary life extremely well; we ought to forgive those few who are pursuing other, higher goals and who live for and understand those alone. Beethoven was one of these. He needed tender care, like a child, yet those who sought to care for him had to remain invisible, anonymous benefactors, of whose ministra-

tions he would barely be conscious.
Beethoven lived for mankind in general, not for the individual. The rest of us should have sensed this, should have ignored or overcome our personal feelings, approaching him with goodwill and dignity. To be sure, this is asking much, but Beethoven could not be dealt with in any other way.

One is reminded of the self-defeating, suspicious attitude of Tasso, as Goethe represented him [Goethe, *Torquato Tasso*; see, for instance, Act I, scene 2]. Surely we applaud the magnanimous Alphonso and the fatherly way in which he deals with the sick

Tasso. By loving a great artist without reservation or conditions one can share in his fame — indeed, one has a share in his work as an artist and in his creation of beauty.

Beethoven's way of working did not fit the conventions of a regulated household, so that either he or his patron would have had to make some adjustment; yet neither was able to do so. As I have mentioned in my Mozart biography, Beethoven liked to compose outdoors: there he could best find ideas. When they came, he treasured them as the inspirations of the moment but did not concern himself with developing them immediately. While still outdoors, however, he would commit them to paper and would continue them on his way home and once at home. Only the working out of these ideas in score was carried out in his room, and even that he preferred to do outdoors when possible. These habits could hardly fit in with a household routine. How could Beethoven, while in his heaven, think about mealtime? Only when he had returned to earth would he desire mortal nourishment. But those who had remained below could hardly be expected to put up with his forgetting, or to await his return.

At this time Beethoven's compositions were as much appreciated in Vienna as elsewhere, but his virtuosity as a pianist was esteemed even more highly. Indeed he was then a greater performer than composer. Whenever he agreed to play, in private circles or in public concerts, it was an important event. People marveled at the facility with which he executed difficult passages. His playing may not always have been delicate, and at times may have lacked clarity, but it was extremely brilliant. He excelled particularly at free improvisation. Here it was really quite extraordinary with what ease, and yet soundness in the succession of ideas, he would improvise on any theme given to him, not just varying the theme in his fingers but really developing it. In this he resembled Mozart more than any other modern artist.[39] Everyone vied to have Beethoven attend their social events; and the gratitude he received must have endeared Vienna to him.

This is why he declined the offer of a position in England, where his compositions were regarded even more highly than in Germany.[40] His income would have been better than in Vienna, but it was uncertain whether life in England would be as enjoyable, and things were cheaper in Vienna. Moreover, two brothers had followed him to Austria. The proximity of family members gave him the kind of happiness he cherished most.

Because of the war the arts endured much, and this caused Beethoven's circumstances to change. He now saw the advantages of a position that would guarantee him a steady income. He had also suffered a great disappointment in an affair of the heart (suffering that is clearly reflected in his compositions of the period), which increased his dissatisfaction with his situation.[41] He therefore considered it a stroke of luck when in 1809 Jerome Bonaparte, then King of Westphalia, offered him the court Kapellmeister position.[42] This, however, gave rise to developments that made it possible for Beethoven to remain in Vienna. People begged him to stay and showered him with favors, so that he did not have the heart to leave. Furthermore, two princes, Lobkowitz and Kinsky, agreed to pay him a fixed yearly salary. They were great patrons of the arts; unfortunately they died early. These two high-minded noblemen were joined by a third — a member of the imperial family, whose name is held in awe by patriots and music lovers alike: His Imperial Highness, Archduke Rudolph, Cardinal and Archbishop of Olmütz. Beethoven was to receive from the three a lifetime stipend of 2000 gulden per annum, with the sole condition (truly an honor) that he would always remain in Austria.[43]

Such favorable arrangements made it possible for Beethoven to live without material worries, all the more so since he also received honoraria from his publishers and at times substantial gifts from those to whom he had dedicated compositions.

His art brought him many other accolades and distinctions. After his masterwork *The Battle of Vittoria* was performed for the Congress of Vienna, the Russian empress (now deceased, but ever to be honored) sent him 200 ducats as an expression of her thanks.[44] In England a group of people sent Beethoven as a gift a fortepiano from the shop of the foremost instrument maker there,[45] while the Vienna city council, in recognition of his accomplishments, made Beethoven an honorary citizen.[46]

Soon after he reached adulthood, Beethoven's hearing, so excellent in his youth, began to diminish. The deterioration was minimal at first but continually worsened. All efforts to locate and deal with the affliction's source were futile. The probable cause was the unusual sensitivity of the various parts of his hearing mechanism: the more it was used, the worse the problem grew. Eventually the condition became so bad that all conversation became impossible. When an ear trumpet proved inadequate and actually caused him physical pain, writing became the only way of communicating with him. In view of his deafness, his continued ability to compose seems miraculous. His piano playing, however, declined, losing its earlier precision. Although Beethoven never had a pleasing singing voice, his speech had always been clear, but it too now betrayed his deafness as his voice became somewhat raucous.[47]

When his deafness became noticeable, Beethoven began avoiding all large gatherings. He only socialized with close friends whose lips he could read. The piano too was neglected and he lived almost exclusively for composing, with the occasional diversion provided by historical studies. Seldom did he complain about the solitude that his ailment had forced upon him.

Nor was he truly lonesome; his active and versatile mind provided him with his own kind of social life.

To every discerning person it was immediately apparent that Beethoven was a remarkable human being. His walk was animated, his mouth was expressive, and his eyes betrayed the enormous depth of his feelings. But it was his magnificent forehead that revealed his majestic creative force.[*]

---

[*]Once at a social gathering a lady expressed admiration for his forehead. Beethoven was not insensitive to such compliments and replied: "Well, then, go ahead and plant a kiss on this forehead!" This the charming lady did not hesitate to do.

When he displayed a friendly mien it had the charm of childlike innocence; when he smiled one believed not only in him but in all mankind. At such times his every word, motion, and glance seemed sincere and genuine.[48]

It has been claimed that Beethoven lacked education — a statement that is unfounded. "Education" is a word so often used in daily life that one tends to lose sight of its true meaning. Beethoven was not courtly, refined, or polished; he could be somewhat cynical. But this can also be said of Lessing and his language, or of the great Caesar, concerning the way he

Pencil drawing of Beethoven by Johann Peter
Theodor Lyser, c.1823. Courtesy Gesellschaft
der Musikfreunde, Vienna.

lived. Beethoven may not have read Chesterfield's letters or Knigge's book on etiquette,[49] nor lived according to their postulates, but he was not un-educated.

He was very perceptive in forming his opinions and frequently expressed them with biting, even coarse humor, until his poor hearing began to inter-fere with conversation. Often he would mention only a single key word per-taining to an anecdote, believing that it was sufficient to convey his meaning. Those who were unfamiliar with the anecdote, or did not immediately catch the allusion, would be puzzled, but those who caught on would quickly burst into laughter.

Most anecdotes he quoted were based on what he had read in the Leipziger musikalische Zeitung. For instance, if he wanted to indicate his displeasure with a singer who performed poorly on the stage, he might turn to someone sitting next to him and say quite audibly: "Da capo." The remark goes back to the following incident. In Paris, a mediocre singer, with a weak voice, slight chest, and so forth, performed an interminable bravura aria. Everyone longed for it to end. It finally did, and the singer was roundly

booed. Only one person in the audience called out, "Da capo!" [encore].
The singer, listening only to that one
voice, bowed humbly and gratefully
repeated the entire aria, though he
could hardly hear himself because of
the ensuing uproar in the house. When
he ended, the hissing and booing was
worse than before, but as it died down,
the same low male voice shouted very
loudly again, "Da capo!" Indeed, the
singer bowed once more and launched
into the aria for the third time. The
other listeners were about to turn
against the man who had caused all the
trouble, when he exclaimed: "Je vou-

lais fair créver cette can[aille]!" (I was hoping the wretch would sing himself to death!)

If, during a performance, the public in the gallery became too noisy, Beethoven would say: "The sacrificial beasts." Why? He had read the following story in the Musikalische Zeitung. A certain person took a visitor to a theater where the audience on the main floor became extremely unruly, stamping their feet, shouting, and ranting. The noise frightened the visitor, who thought there was a fire. The host calmed him down, but his companion exclaimed: "How can such howling be tolerated in a theater, a temple of good taste?" "These are the sacrificial beasts," was the reply.

Kapellmeister Benda[*] once, while on a journey, looked in on his old friend, music director Rust in Dessau.[50] This fine person, a sensitive soul, was overjoyed to see Benda. It was midday, and Rust served the best possible meal, accompanied by much triv-

---

[*]Georg Benda, born in 1721 [1722] in Jungbunzlau [Staré Benátky], died 6 November 1795 in Köstritz. He was the director of music to the Duke of Gotha and composed many works distinguished by their expressive power, noblest melody, and purest harmony.

ial chatter. Though he loved Rust dearly, Benda was happily concentrating on the dinner, so he let Rust talk while he paid attention to the good wine.

"Tell me, where do you obtain this excellent wine?" Benda asked earnestly, as they rose from the table. "From —s in Bremen. But now, my friend, I'll take you to the delightful garden residence of the princess, and on our way there I'll tell you all about the joys and sorrows I have experienced during the fourteen years since I last saw you." Benda, who was walking ahead, heard none of this. At last they arrive at the princess's villa, and as they enter, Benda returns down to earth, as it were. Well, he thinks, I must have been dreaming for a few minutes! What bad manners! I must make up for it and resume our conversation where my dreaming interrupted it. "So, from Bremen!"

Even while he could still hear well, Beethoven, like Benda, was apt to get lost in his own thoughts while ostensibly conversing with others. He would then apologize, usually saying, "So, from Bremen!" Those who understood the joke would forgive him, but others must have been puzzled.

He was also fond of telling entire anecdotes when the occasion presented itself. Like Mozart, Beethoven was incensed by the German adulation of Italian singers, and he became enraged when they were worshipped in spite of their arrogance. This once happened in Vienna, where a certain Italian singer's bad manners were put up with again and again. People accepted her complaints that she had not been honored enough, though she had been feted far more than her singing warranted and was not above leaving a party without having sung, even when the guests had been invited especially to hear her. Even so, the Viennese would forgive her.

Beethoven sought to have her see her shameful behavior by telling several anecdotes about Caffarelli. He had them extracted from the Musikalische Zeitung and distributed copies:

The castrato Caffarelli,* though not the inventor, was the first to champion the

---

*Gaetano Majorano, called Caffarelli, was the son of a poor peasant. In 1760 he bought a dukedom, which entitled him to call himself Duca di Santo dorato, a title later inherited by his nephew. In spite of this success, he continued to accumulate money by singing in churches and monasteries. At his death in Naples in 1783 his fortune, also inherited by his nephew, yielded an annual

embellishments, coloraturas, and variations that characterize modern Italian
singing. No singer in the world surpasses
him in vocal dexterity and in executing
the most graceful and elaborate vocal
ornaments. With these he held the public
spellbound and almost destroyed the
nobler Italian tradition of singing as
taught by Porpora. He was showered
with so much applause and gold that
he could buy a dukedom. His diamond
jewelry alone was worth more than two
million livres. As he grew richer he
became exceedingly vain, proud, and
temperamental.

He went to Paris where he sang for

---

income of 12,000 ducats, mostly derived
from land he had bought. He built a man-
sion for himself; over the portal he put the
inscription *Amphion Thebas, Ego domum.*[51]

King Louis XV and his court. In appreciation, the king sent him a precious golden box. "What!" Caffarelli shouted at the messenger, "the king sends me such a box? Keep it: I already have thirty others that are worth more than this one. If it at least were decorated with the king's portrait — '' "Sir," the messenger replied, "the King of France presents his portrait only to ambassadors." "Bah — ambassadors? Then let him invite ambassadors to sing for him!"

When the king heard of this he laughed and reported the incident to the Dauphin's wife, the Princess of Saxony, herself a great music lover. She summoned the singer, mentioned nothing about his impertinence, and gave him a beautiful diamond along with a passport, saying, "It's signed by the king himself — a great honor for you! But you'd better use it right now, for it is valid for only ten days."

Caffarelli then went to Rome. Cardinal Albani invited him, along with ladies and gentlemen of the highest society. Caffarelli accepted the invitation and promised to sing, even sending ahead the music for one of his most popular arias.

The evening, the very hour of the concert came, but no Caffarelli. When the cardinal sent a messenger, he found the singer in his dressing gown and slippers. "What has happened? His Eminence and Rome's first families are waiting for you!" exclaimed the perplexed messenger. "Oh, *che disgrazia!*" (what a pity!) replied the virtuoso. "I quite forgot. Ask His Eminence to excuse me; I'll come some other time. I am not feeling well, and besides, by the time I readied myself, the evening would be over. As I said, ask him to excuse me. Another time!"

When informed of this, the assembled luminaries were stunned. Albani quickly decided how to proceed: he ordered his major-domo to take a coach to Caffarelli's, with four well-built servants following him on horseback. On arrival, the major-domo addressed the singer: "Sir, you are to come with me to the cardinal just as you are." Caffarelli remonstrated, the four sturdy servants made some slight but unmistakable gestures, and the major-domo, in a cold, firm voice, repeated his demand. Nonplussed, the singer complied. Arriving at the palace, he entered the brilliant hall in his robe and slippers. He tried, with gestures and a few stammered words, to make excuses: no one said a word or moved.

His burly companions turn to the left, taking him to the orchestra. Deathly silence prevails. He is escorted to his music stand: no chair in sight, let alone the seat of honor to which he had become accustomed. As soon as he reaches his music stand, the orchestra begins to play. To his dismay, it is the introduction to his aria. Whether he wanted to or not, Caffarelli was forced to sing, and in spite of his resentment he sang quite well. Loud applause followed, with shouts of "Bravo Caffarelli!"

Silence then returned, as did the five threatening figures who ordered him to proceed to the anteroom. There the major-domo presented him with a magnificent box filled with coins, saying, "Please accept from His Eminence this reward for your talent." To which the four horsemen added: "And now accept this reward from His Eminence for your insolence!" With that, each of them gave him a mighty blow with his horsewhip. When the guests in the adjoining salon heard his yelling and cursing, they resumed their shouting: "Bravo Caffarelli!"

The next day one of the favorite sayings in town was that the cardinals were better taskmasters than the French kings.

As I said, Beethoven had copies made of these anecdotes, which were copied again.[52] Predictably, one of these was steered to the aforementioned prima donna, in the hope that she might mend her arrogant ways. In this way, Beethoven's action affected not only the present but also the future.

I mentioned earlier that on occasion Beethoven could be somewhat cynical, though not in the usually accepted sense of the word. The way he used this anecdote illustrates the kind of cynicism I have in mind.

Beethoven's dress was always immaculate, especially his linen.[53] He did not dress extravagantly and was not interested in the latest fashions, but neither did he wish to look old-fashioned. His living quarters were also very clean. What offended some people was that they were not well appointed or as tidy as they had expected. Beethoven was not concerned with such matters, still less with expensive furnishings. Since he was fond of working in the open air, he moved to the countryside every spring and returned to the city only in late fall. With this constant moving it is no wonder that it took a long time for his belongings to be put in order, especially his papers. Expensive furniture was out of the question since his frequent moves kept him from leasing a city apartment for any length of time. He only wanted comfortable furnishings, and since they were not in bad taste, most people were satisfied by them.[54]

Great as Beethoven's art was, his heart was yet greater.[55] It was filled with an ineradicable loathing of hypocrisy, obsequiousness, vanity, and avarice; he objected to the superficiality of most people's lifestyles. Those who shared these feelings readily recognized him as a man in the fullest sense. His attachment to his family was one of his most attractive qualities. He did all he could to help his two brothers who had moved to Austria. One of them had become a public servant; when he died, Beethoven took in his son and spared no expense to provide him with the best education, even at the cost of his own peace of mind and happy disposition.[56]

He also sought to help others. He performed several of his compositions to help worthy institutions and supported especially the poor of the Bürgerspital.

In his early years Beethoven enjoyed good health, but late in life it was undermined by serious heart disease that, during his last six months, necessitated medical treatment.[57] Though this alleviated the illness, it did not cure him. Eventually dropsy developed, causing much pain, which Beethoven accepted with equanimity. He was consoled by expressions of sympathy from many places, including England. From there a group of people sent him a substantial sum of money, urging him to use it for the best possible care;[58] they also instructed their Vienna bank to make available additional funds if needed. Some German newspapers interpreted this as an indictment of the Viennese, who supposedly had shirked their responsibilities, causing the need for help from abroad. These accusations were unjust, for Beethoven did not lack good care. It is, to be sure, to the credit of the English that they also wanted to help. An artist does not belong to one place but to the entire world.

Beethoven faced death with equanimity. He willed his estate to his nephew, appointing Court Councillor von Breuning, a longtime friend, as his guardian. But Breuning also died before long.[59] Beethoven left only 4000 gulden in cash. Considering how little he spent on himself this was a small sum; there would have been much more if he had not helped his family so substantially.[60]

Chest pains increased his suffering during his last days, but he died peacefully on 26 March 1827. The Viennese gave appropriate expression to the painful loss suffered by art and by all mankind; it was shared not only by the German-speaking countries but by all of Europe.

Friends defrayed the cost of the funeral so that the nephew's inheritance would not be diminished.[61] The funeral took place on 29 March; mourners from all ranks of society formed the cortege that moved from Beethoven's home in the Alser suburb to the nearby church where the consecration of the body took place. This procession took almost an hour, passing through huge crowds of spectators. All were in deepest mourning, and their great silence was interrupted only by the sighs of the poor who had lost their benefactor.

From the church the cortege proceeded to the beautiful Währing Cemetery. No one left it at the church; all continued on to the burial site, where

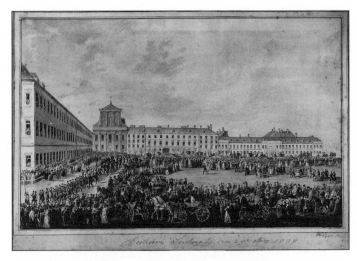

Beethoven's funeral procession,
watercolor by Franz Stöber, 1827.
Courtesy Beethoven-Haus, Bonn.

an oration by the venerable Grillparzer
was read by Anschütz, Vienna's foremost actor.[62] It was delivered most
movingly from the elevated entrance,
to those assembled below. I am in-

cluding the text of the oration, as already printed in several journals:[63]

As we stand here by the grave of the dear departed, we represent, in a way, the entire nation, all German people. We mourn the loss of one highly celebrated half of what has been left to us of the former splendor of our native art, of the fatherland's spiritual flowering. To be sure, the hero of German melodious poetry [Goethe] still lives, and long may he live! But the master of tuneful song, the heir and amplifier of the immortal fame of Handel and Bach, of Haydn and Mozart, has expired, and we weep as we stand by the broken strings of the silent harp.

The silent harp! Let me call him thus! For he was an artist, and became what he was through art alone. Life had dealt him cruel blows, and just as he who has been shipwrecked clings to the shore, so he sought refuge in your arms — in divine art, the glorious sister of the good and the true, who consoles the suffering. He clung to you, and even after the door through which you had first reached him had closed, you spoke to him. Though his deafness caused him to become blind to your features, he still carried your image in his heart, and when he died this image still rested on his breast.

He was an artist, and who can stand up beside him? As the behemoth storms through the seas, he rushed on to the limits of his art. From the cooing of the dove to the rolling of thunder, from the very ingenious interweaving of the most intractable elements of art, to that dreaded point where design borders on the arbitrary lawlessness of contending forces of nature, he had grasped and experienced it all. Whoever comes after him will not be able to continue on his path;

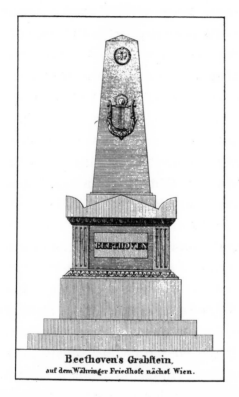

Beethoven's gravestone at Währing Cemetery,
unsigned engraving sold by Tobias Haslinger.
Courtesy Gesellschaft der Musikfreunde,
Vienna.

he must begin anew, for his predecessor left off only where art itself leaves off.

Adelaide and Leonore! Celebration of the heroes of Vittoria, and devout sacrificial song of the Mass! Children of song in three and four voices! Raging symphony! And you, the swan song, *Freude, schöner Götterfunken*! Muse of song and of the lyre! Gather around his grave and adorn it with laurel! He was an artist, but also a man — a human being in the word's most perfect sense. Because he withdrew from the world they called him hostile, and because he shunned sentimentality they said he lacked feeling. But no: he who knows himself to be firm does not flee. He who is oversensitive avoids the display of feeling. If he fled from the world, it was because in the depths of his loving nature there was no weapon to defend himself against it. If he withdrew from mankind it was because he had given his all and received nothing in return. He remained alone because he did not find a second self.

Yet to the end he opened his heart to all men, offering fatherly affection to those close to him, and his possessions, indeed his blood, to the world. This is how he was and how he died, and thus will he live for all time.

You, however, who have followed our funeral procession thus far, overcome your grief. You have not lost him, you have won him. He lives! When the door of life closes behind us, the portals open to the temple of immortality. There he now stands, among the great of all time, inviolate forever.

Part from here, therefore, grieving but composed. And if ever the force of his creations overwhelms you like an onrushing tempest, when your tears flow amid a generation as yet unborn, then

remember this hour and think: we were
there when they buried him, and when
he died, we wept.

Tears were still seen to fall as people returned home; and the continuing
silence confirmed that they wanted to
preserve the deep impression made by
the words of the speech.

During the following days several
music societies performed three Re-
quiems in memory of the deceased.
The first, in St. Augustine's Church,
featured Mozart's Requiem; the other
two employed Cherubini's,[64] heard in
St. Charles's and in St. Augustine's.
These were masterful performances,

Franz Grillparzer (1791–1872), by Michael
Daffinger, 1827. Courtesy Gesellschaft der
Musikfreunde, Vienna.

greatly moving the large, prayerful audiences, which were made up of people from all walks of life.

On 1 May it was traditional to give a concert in the Augarten, to welcome the return of the greenery of spring. Herr Schuppanzigh, a member of the Imperial and Royal Court Chapel,[65] was in charge of these fine occasions; this year he began and ended the concert with works by Beethoven, adding to the significance of the celebration. The first composition heard was the great symphony in B-flat major; the most recent overture in C major concluded the program.[66]

Concert hall in the Augarten, unsigned
engraving, c.1820. Courtesy Gesellschaft der
Musikfreunde, Vienna.

Even more significant was the assembly featuring music and poetry
presented on 4 May by members of the
Concerts Spirituels, an organization

founded by Franz Xaver Gebauer and continued by Herr Piringer.[67] The event took place in the Provincial Assembly Hall and, with the exception of one excellent poem, consisted entirely of works by Beethoven: 1) Fifth great symphony in C minor; 2) *Beethoven*, a poem by Johann Gabriel Seidl, recited by Herr Anschütz, actor at the Court Theater; 3) First movement of Beethoven's Violin Concerto, performed by Professor J. Böhm; 4) *Adelaide*, sung by Herr Ludwig Tietze; 5) First movement of the C minor piano concerto, played by Herr Carl Maria von Bocklet; and 6) Chorus from the oratorio

Christ on the Mount of Olives.[68] The concert succeeded magnificently, but its purpose was even more praiseworthy. The box-office receipts and other larger contributions were to be used for the creation of a monument for the deceased, a project of which the aforementioned Councillor [Stephan] von Breuning had taken charge. Expenses of the concert were not subtracted from the total receipts. Other musical organizations will sponsor similar concerts, so that this objective will be accomplished quickly for Beethoven, whereas in spite of noble and protracted efforts it has not yet been accomplished for

Haydn and Mozart, and will now again become my concern.

I have offered a prize for the best proposals for Haydn's and Mozart's monuments, and I intend to do the same for Beethoven's. We know that one of the contestants will be Herr Schärmer, highly regarded for his historical paintings and portraits. He became famous through his design of Hofer's monument, which won the prize offered by the Imperial-Royal Academy of Fine Arts. With such an artist among the contestants we can be sure that the project will be beautifully realized.

There already exist examples of a union of music and the visual arts to commemorate Beethoven. Thus Herr Joseph Kern, court silversmith whose shop is at Kohlmarkt No. 257, has created a most handsome silver medallion depicting Beethoven. Also, the famous sculptor Anton Dietrich, Auf der Wieden No. 277, has created two marble busts, from life.[69] Dietrich had previously sculpted very lifelike busts of His Majesty the Austrian Emperor, and of Goethe, Schiller, Richter, and others; these had established his excellent reputation. He has received frequent requests from abroad for [bronze] copies of his Beethoven busts, which have also been praised in several newspapers. These marble effigies and their copies are meant for display not only in concert halls but also on pianos in private homes, just as has been done with busts of Haydn and Mozart created by his teacher, Vienna's master sculptor, Director Klieber.

To the literary tributes of Grillparzer and Seidl we can add a beautiful poem by Kanne,[70] published by Tendler and von Manstein, and an affectionate song with piano accompaniment by Joseph Drechsler, with text by Castelli. It has been published by Diabelli.[71]

Everything, then, was done in Vienna to pay highest tribute to Beethoven, in the name of the German nation. The manner in which he was commemorated and honored in Prague was also most impressive. Like the Austrians, the inhabitants of Bohemia were eager to honor Beethoven for his accomplishments in the art of music. A choir of nearly a hundred singers participated in solemn exequies in Prague's St. Nicholas Church, in the center of which an illuminated catafalque had been erected. This service took place on 27 July. The singers, under the direction of Vincenz Mašek, the highly esteemed dean of Bohemian composers, were divided into three choirs.[72] They performed three choral works composed for the occasion,* along with the Libera by Ignaz Ritter

---

*The first specially composed work was a Requiem by Joseph Schubert, first violinist at this church; the second a Benedictus by Albin Mašek; and the third a choral prayer with text and music by Aloys Gelen, a fine singer and Mašek's pupil. This composition expresses Bohemia's sincere and great love for and veneration of Beethoven. Seyfried's Libera had been written for the funeral; the Miserere, based on a Beethoven manuscript, had been adapted and furnished with a text by Seyfried.[73]

Anton Diabelli (1781–1858), lithograph
by Josef Kriehuber, 1841. Courtesy
Gesellschaft der Musikfreunde, Vienna.

von Seyfried and Beethoven's own Miserere.

The choral music was splendidly performed; it was so appropriate to the occasion that the large audience, which came from all segments of the population, was greatly moved.

Let us hope that these events will be an incentive, both here and abroad, to fulfill in the same way our obligation to the two greater predecessors of Beethoven, who deserve our gratitude to an even higher degree. To fail in this duty would indeed be cause for censure.

Assessments
of
Beethoven's Works

I shall not give a detailed list of Beethoven's works,* since all establishments selling music have catalogs that include such a list. Nevertheless, it may be useful to provide here some thoughts about these works and their merit.

In the life of every great artist we can discern distinct periods. These are

---

*I shall, however, provide such a list in a later supplement to this biography, which will be available free of charge to all subscribers.[74]

necessary steps in his development, following certain strong natural forces and laws. Some masters display an unquestionable perfection from the beginning — but their early efforts were not made public, so that their real beginnings are not known to us. They may later become interested in different subject matter; such a change also signals a transition to the next stage of artistic development. This is especially true of Goethe, whose artistic career, in its entirety, demonstrates the broad scope of a single creative force.

Our intention is to indicate the various stages Beethoven passed through in his career in order to arrive at his unique and ultimate perfection. In determining these stages one must not go solely by the numbers assigned to his works, for some were written early but published later.[75] Nor should we expect such an account to be mathematically precise, for music is an effusion of artistic freedom.

Beethoven's genius first manifested itself in three trios for piano, violin, and cello.[76] They display extraordinarily deep sentiments, which have not yet found their true outlet. This has caused some to complain of disorder in these and some subsequent compositions, and not without reason. In these and some later works Beethoven reveals his heart, in a great surge of feeling. With this music we enter a new world, which he was to conquer triumphantly. At this early stage his nature could express itself only in grand proportions, not always clearly realized but already sharply distinctive. The expressive melodies found in the Allegros and outstandingly beautiful Adagios especially caused connoisseurs to have great expectations.

Considering the grand and passionate style of his music, it is natural that he demanded more than what was

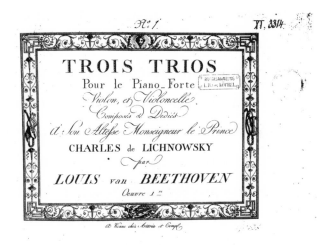

Piano Trios, Op. 1. Title page of first edition.
Courtesy Gesellschaft der Musikfreunde,
Vienna.

usually required from his instruments.
He also made significant contributions
to the technique of piano playing,
expanding it with several effective de-

vices. For instance, he relied on broken, arpeggiated harmonic accompaniment far more than had been customary.

Beethoven's works of this and the next period remind us, through their formal structure, of Haydn and Mozart, but Beethoven, though still influenced by these masters, gradually achieved an independent, distinct style of his own. The famous sextet belongs to this period, as do the C major and D major symphonies, and the 16 [=6] string quartets of Opus 18.[77] But these are works of a maturing artist, so that not surprisingly they contain many hints of the later period.

His works from opus numbers 40 to 60 are transitional, though not consistently so, for there is an occasional looking back to earlier times. An example of music from this period is the *Sinfonia eroica.*[78] Generally speaking, works from this period are very serious but interrupted at times by boisterous merriment. This occurs when an artist's superabundant creative force erupts into mischievous, spirited banter; we can conveniently call it musical humor. If one is allowed a conjecture, it seems that the character of several works from this period shows the composer in a frame of mind induced by unusual events or circumstances, as I suggested earlier.

Beethoven's Fifth Symphony impressively signals the onset of his third period.[79] With its combination of retrospective and prophetic sounds, it represents the inner life of the artist. It opens with a fiery Allegro; its serious mood, setting the overall tone, speaks of a powerful life. The Andante that follows, though sad and mournful, nevertheless offers a confident glimpse of eternity. An Allegro then suggests the outbreak of the storm of fate, but with the start of the Finale all earthly bonds are broken, freeing the spirit to soar high under the sun's bright rays of eternal freedom.

The works of this last period are shaped by inner necessity. Everything follows organically from what preceded, so that everything accidental, uncertain, or extraneous is excluded. Thus each composition constitutes a meaningful, coherent, and unified whole. In the same way, the fruit emerges from the blossom, which itself owes its life to the growing tree: that is the mysterious law of life, in nature and in art. In his composing Beethoven seems to respond to a creative imperative that governs everything, to the smallest detail. He may proceed from an ordinary, even insignificant theme, and explore, spin out, or develop all its inherent possibilities. This is easily overlooked by those who cannot comprehend an art form that is complete in itself. In this we can compare Beethoven to Goethe. Like that great man, he sometimes begins with an unpromising subject, but its treatment, down to the smallest detail, reveals a truly original spirit.

So much for Beethoven's works in general. It is always extremely difficult to discuss art of any kind in appropriate, meaningful terms. Any evalua-

GRAND QUATUOR

en Partition

pour

deux Violons, Alto et Violoncelle,

composé et dedié

à Son Altesse Monseigneur le Prince

Nicolas de Galitzin,

Lieutenant-Colonel de la Garde S. M. I. de toutes les Russies,

par

LOUIS v. BEETHOVEN.

Oeuv. 127.

N° 2426. ——————— Propriété des Editeurs. ——————— Pr. 2 fl. 36 kr.

Mayence, chez B. Schott Fils.

Quartet, Op. 127. Title page of first edition.

tions must be based on considered, unemotional judgment, but then they must be phrased in poetic language, for beauty can only be explained adequately in terms of beauty. Surely no one thinks that art, the manifestation of a free spirit, can be contained in some dank, unsuitable chamber under lock and key.

This applies especially to music: the greater its powerful message, the more spontaneously a sensitive person will respond to it. After experiencing a wealth of emotions, the individual retains only joyful reverence for that which cannot be expressed in words.

Such a person would hardly wish to transform the poetic experience of a precious moment into the dry prose of critical language. That wish may arise later, but by then memory may have faded, and one may look in vain for the right words to express what is in one's heart. Then the chosen words may be inadequate to describe a glorious experience that ended all too soon.

Let us therefore refrain from attempting to describe Beethoven's innermost nature, for the reasons just given. His music itself will be the banner under which a growing number of disciples will gather. They will be united by their common admiration of the master; they will form a circle where all know each other — a union that cannot and need not be described.

A few miscellaneous observations may be appropriate at this point.

In his vocal music, Beethoven's overflowing enthusiasm kept him at times from paying close attention to the words. They merely surround the music like a loosely fitting garment, which he occasionally sheds altogether.[80] This is not to excuse the occasionally improper fit of his texts, and certainly does not recommend it. Rather we ask for a little forbearance, mindful of the great, consummate music he wrote in spite of this peculiarity. Every artist must expect to face rigorous criticism, but instead of ignoring the artist's individuality the critic must try to explain it satisfactorily in terms of generally valid principles.

The opera *Fidelio* has succeeded wherever it has been well performed;[81] it should not be judged frivolously. The listener who approaches it seriously and with reverence will surely be richly rewarded.

It would be fortunate for Beethoven and for music if someone had the inclination and talent to explore and understand the composer's manner of expression and would then supply the broad outlines of a text. Until that has been done it is premature to judge Beethoven's abilities in that regard.

Whoever is very fond of a certain kind of music will try to relate it to its sources and models. Thus it seems natural to compare Mozart and Beethoven. The former delights us by the perfection of execution; the latter excels by the grandiose concept of his creations. Beethoven displays more passion; Mozart's music provides a wealth of inner satisfaction. Mozart, through his music, expresses what he

Playbill for the first performance of the first version of *Fidelio*, 20 November 1805 at the Theater an der Wien.

wants to be at that time; Beethoven conveys what he *must* be — from strength, not weakness. In Mozart great artistic freedom prevails, while Beethoven composes out of an inner necessity, a kind of musical predestination. In listening to him we might imagine that his music comes down to us from higher spheres, learned from demonic forces, and that he passes it on to us, though constrained by the oppressive atmosphere of our earthly realm.[*]

---

[*]In his letters from Vienna, Reichardt has the following to say on Beethoven's relation to Haydn and Mozart: "Haydn created the

When Beethoven composes he is not always correct, but it is evident that he could be if he so desired. One should not reproach him for this any

---

string quartet, drawing from the pure well-spring of his own serene, original personality. No one displays more childlike qualities or more mirth. Mozart's forceful nature and richer imagination went farther afield; some of his works explore the highest and lowest realms of his inner being. He was more of a performing virtuoso; therefore he made far greater technical demands on his players. He put more emphasis on complex, artful development, expanding Haydn's lovely garden cottage into a palace. Beethoven soon felt at home in this palace. In order to express his own nature in distinctive ways it remained for him to construct a daring high tower, but anyone attempting to add to the tower's height would risk his neck."[82]

more than one censures Shakespeare for certain errors. Neither Beethoven's nor Shakespeare's creations are out of character because of this; in this regard our composer is entirely blameless.[83]

Those who admire Bach comprehend Beethoven most readily, for the two are kindred spirits. But there are many educated people who have only a general understanding of music, or are too much tied to conventional form. They cannot comprehend Beethoven's music, which is so very free and original.

Some of his late works have met with hostility because of performances that were almost always inadequate. For a real understanding of his music one must study the scores.

By way of elaborating on an earlier remark there follow a few slightly modified verses by Schiller. They describe Beethoven's music fairly well.

Ein Regenstrom aus Felsenrissen,
Er kommt mit Donners Ungestüm,
Bergtrümmer folgen seinen Güssen
Und Eichen stürzen unter ihm.
Erstaunt mit wollustvollem Grausen
Hört ihn der Wanderer und lauscht,
Er hört die Fluth vom Felsen brausen,
Doch weiss er nicht, woher sie rauscht.
So strömen seiner Töne Wellen
Hervor aus nie entdeckten Quellen.

Torrential rains spout from rocky crevices,
accompanied by fierce thunder.
Avalanches of boulders follow,
tearing down large oak trees.
The wanderer, both fascinated and
    horrified,
hears the torrential floods
as they roar down from the cliffs,
but he does not know from whence they
    come.
Thus the flood of his music
streams forth from never-fathomed
    sources.[84]

Postscript

A supplement to this biography will be published as soon as I know what funds are needed for the construction of a Haydn monument. This supplement will consist of

a) a detailed drawing of the monument, with legend and further information about the monument's erection, and so on;

b) a complete catalog of Beethoven's works; and

c) the names and titles of all subscribers, with the number of copies ordered by each.

Those who generously supported the undertaking, by soliciting subscriptions themselves or in other ways, will be specially and gratefully mentioned. Immediately after publication all subscribers to this biography will receive this supplement free of charge through the appropriate bookstores, post offices, or newspaper distributors. Therefore subscribers are requested to give their full name, title, and address. Their names, as subscribers and as supporters of the monument, will be printed at the beginning of the supplement. The addresses are also needed for its delivery.

It should also be noted that a second volume will soon appear, entitled *Züge und Anecdoten aus Beethovens Leben* [Vignettes and Anecdotes from Beethoven's Life]. It will also serve as a supplement to the biography itself.[85]

The Author.

[Vienna], 6 February 1826

My esteemed and most worthy Sir!

You have really performed a very good deed by rendering justice to the shades of Mozart in your truly masterly work, which is such a penetrating study of the subject. Both lay and profane people and all who are at all musical or can even be accounted such must feel indebted to you —

Either no talent whatever or a very great one is required to produce what H[err] W[eber] has produced. Let us bear in mind too that, so far as I remember, this person has written a book on composition and yet tries to attribute to Mozart passages like

And if we add an example of W[eber]'s own clumsy work, such as[86]

then when appreciating H[err] W[eber]'s extraordinary knowledge of harmony and melody, we are reminded of the former old Imperial composers Sterkel, Haueisen, Kalkbrenner (I mean the father), Andre (but by no means the other one) and so forth.[87]

Requiescant in pace [may they rest in peace] — But I am particularly grateful to you, my esteemed friend, for the pleasure you have given me by sending me your treatise. For I have always counted myself among the greatest admirers of Mozart and shall remain so until my last breath — [88]

Reverend sir, *I will very soon ask you for your blessing* —

With sincere regards, most worthy sir, I remain yours faithfully

Notes

1. Joseph Haydn (1732–1809) was Beethoven's teacher from the time of the latter's arrival in Vienna in November 1792 until Haydn's departure for England in January 1794.
2. Conradin Kreutzer (1780–1849) was a composer and conductor, unrelated to the famous violinist Rodolphe Kreutzer. He became Kapellmeister to Prince Carl Egon II of Fürstenberg at Donaueschingen in 1818, but this appointment became largely nominal after his return to Vienna in 1822. He knew Beethoven and took part in the first performance of the latter's Ninth Symphony in 1824, before moving to Paris in 1827 and back to Vienna in 1829. He was also present at Beethoven's funeral.
3. The first ten lines refer to Beethoven; the last six are addressed to Kreutzer. Transcription of the German poem: Bedarf es gleich des Denkmahls nicht, / Das ich dem Meister hoher Klänge, / Der nie verhallenden Gesänge, / Durch dieses Werk geweiht; / so spricht / Doch laut sich aus die Dank-

barkeit, / Die ihm mein Herz so willig beut; / Denn was dem Zauber seiner Kunst gelang, / Hat Jeder, so wie ich, empfunden, / D'rum für die wonnevollen Stunden / Sey ihm gebracht Lob, Preis und Dank! / Dich, edler Mann, / Der auf des Ruhmes Bahn / So glänzend vorgeschritten, / Mög' es, darum will ich Dich bitten / Als Opfer meiner Liebe ehren, / Und meine Achtung Dir bewähren!

4. No Beethoven monument was erected in Vienna until 1880; meanwhile one was unveiled in Bonn in 1845.

5. This intention was already being carried out, and Schlosser's biography of Mozart is also dated 1828 (modern edition in Schlosser 1993). Its preface is actually dated 21 March 1827, five days *before* Beethoven's death. No monument ensued as a result, however.

6. This is probably a reference to the legend of Amphion; see note 51.

7. Ernst Ludwig Gerber (1746–1819) is most noted as a music collector and lexicographer. In 1790–92 he published a two-volume *Historisch-biographisches Lexikon der Tonkünstler*, based on a similar musical dictionary by Johann Gottfried Walther

(1732). Gerber's lexicon was amplified by four further volumes in 1812–14 and other addenda, and quickly became a standard reference work of the period (see Gerber, Wessely ed. 1966–77). Some portions of Schlosser's book—for example the accounts of Bach and Handel—are taken almost verbatim from Gerber.

8. No biography of Haydn by Schlosser is known.

9. Josef Kriehuber (1800–1876) produced at least six lithographic portraits of Beethoven after the composer's death. The first (1827) was essentially a portrait of Anton Dietrich's bust itself, but for Schlosser's book the image was transformed into a realistic portrait of the composer, probably with the aid of an 1824 drawing by Stefan Decker (see Steblin 1992, where the three portraits are illustrated, and Letters 1994). See also note 69 below.

10. Abbé Maximilian Stadler (1748–1833) was a priest and composer. He lived in Vienna from 1796 to 1803 and from 1815 until his death, and knew both Beethoven and Schlosser. The letter is reproduced as endpapers to this edition.

11. Stadler's defense of Mozart's Requiem, published as *Vertheidigung der Echtheit des Mozartischen Requiem* (Vienna, 1826) was in response to an article by Gottfried Weber in *Caecilia* (3:205) casting doubt on the work's authenticity. Stadler followed up his defense with two supplements the next year. For a discussion of the Weber-Stadler controversy, see Gärtner 1991, 155–172.

12. Gottfried Weber (1779–1839), not the composer Carl Maria von Weber. Gottfried was the founder and editor of the journal *Caecilia*, and also a theorist and composer, perhaps most noted for having introduced the widely used system of roman numerals to represent chords.

13. Friedrich Schiller (1759–1805), author of *An die Freude*, which Beethoven used in his Ninth Symphony. The quotation has not been identified.

14. Beethoven was actually born in 1770, but for a long time he believed he was born in 1772 and even rejected the evidence of his baptismal certificate, on which he wrote "1772. The baptismal certificate seems to be incorrect" (Thayer, Forbes ed. 1967, 54). Schlosser may have obtained the date

from Gerber's lexicon, which also gives 1772 (see also Solomon 1988, 35–43). The correct date of birth, 16 December 1770, is given on the Kriehuber lithograph that Schlosser reproduced as a frontispiece (and which appears as the frontispiece to this edition) and on Kriehuber's previous lithograph (see note 9). These are among the earliest explicit statements of Beethoven's day of birth, which has caused some controversy (see Albrecht and Schwensen 1988).

15. Beethoven's father was named Johann (c.1740–1792). The only one of Beethoven's close relatives who bore the name Anton was his brother Caspar Anton Carl, whose first two names derived from his sponsor Kaspar Anton Belderbusch; it is possible that this is what caused the mistake, or alternatively someone may have simply confused the two names, which are slightly similar. Maximilian Friedrich was Elector of Cologne from 1761 until his death in 1784.

16. Heinrich Gilles van den Eeden (or der Eden, c.1710–1782).

17. The *Allgemeine musikalische Zeitung* (Gen-

eral Musical Journal) was for many years
the leading German-language music peri-
odical and was regularly read by Beethoven.
Published by Breitkopf & Härtel in Leipzig
from 1798 to 1848, it was initially edited by
Friedrich Rochlitz, who was succeeded by
Gottfried Härtel in 1818. It contained numerous reviews of compositions by Beethoven and of concerts at which his music was
performed. Schlosser refers to it as the
"Leipziger musikalische Zeitung" to distin-
guish it from a Viennese journal with a similar title, published from 1817 to 1824 under
the editorship of Beethoven's friend August
Friedrich Kanne.

18. The violinist and composer Isidore Berthaume (c.1752–1802, not 1801 as given
by Schlosser) was a nephew and pupil of the
violinist Lemière. Schlosser's note is basi-
cally a summary of the entry in Gerber's
lexicon (Gerber, Wessely ed. 1966–77,
2:372), but Gerber correctly gives the date
of Berthaume's death as March 1802.

19. Johann Adam Hiller (1728–1804).

20. Maximilian Franz (1756–1801; ruled
1784–94).

21. The Elector's role here (as also his earlier

alleged payments to van den Eeden for Beethoven's instruction) has been queried by
Thayer (Thayer, Forbes ed. 1967, 60, 64),
who suggests that it was probably Beethoven's father who came to some arrangement
with Neefe concerning the boy's tuition.
However, the Elector would surely have
had to give approval to any such arrangement, which would therefore in a formal
sense have been made on his instructions.

22. This account of Bach is taken almost verbatim from Gerber's lexicon. A few details
are inaccurate—for example, Bach appears
to have composed more church works in
Leipzig than in Weimar.

23. On 2 March 1783, Neefe inserted a notice
about Beethoven in Cramer's *Magazin der
Musik* (1:394), stating that "he plays chiefly
Das wohltemperirte Clavier of Sebastian
Bach, which Herr Neefe put into his hands"
(see Thayer, Forbes ed. 1967, 66). But it
seems unlikely that Beethoven did so before
the age of eleven.

24. No compositions by Beethoven are known
to date from such an early age, but it seems
likely that he did compose something then.

25. Again the information is correct except that

Beethoven's age has been underestimated. His first published composition was the Nine Variations on a March by Ernst Christoph Dressler (WoO 63), published by Götz (Mannheim) in 1782. This was followed in 1783 by the three 'Kurfürsten' Sonatas (WoO 47) and the song *Schilderung eines Mädchens* (WoO 107), and in 1784 by the song *An einen Säugling* (WoO 108), all published by Bossler (Speyer).

26. Carl Ludwig Junker actually heard Beethoven improvise at Mergentheim in autumn 1791, and published an account in Bossler's *Musikalische Correspondenz* in November that year (see Thayer, Forbes ed. 1967, 104–105).

27. Beethoven had already been appointed court organist—alongside Neefe but with a lower salary—in June 1784 (see Thayer-Forbes 1967, 79).

28. Haydn's enthusiasm for Handel's music had been stimulated by Baron van Swieten, who sometimes sponsored performances of Handel oratorios in Vienna, and by a magnificent Handel festival in London that Haydn had attended in May 1791. Haydn was also involved in a performance of *Alexander's*

Feast in Vienna in March 1793 (Landon 1976, 216), and one must assume that Beethoven was present on this occasion.

29. Like Schlosser's account of Bach, this account of Handel is taken straight from Gerber's lexicon and is occasionally inaccurate.

30. Beethoven was actually already familiar with many of Mozart's works, including three operas in which he had taken part in Bonn.

31. Haydn had actually left Vienna for his second visit to London on 19 January 1794. Schlosser's incorrect date is evidently taken from Gerber's lexicon (Gerber, Wessely ed. 1966–77, 2:309; the correct year is given in Gerber's Haydn entry, 2:599).

32. Schlosser's account of Albrechtsberger is taken from Gerber's lexicon (Gerber, Wessely ed. 1966–77, 2:54–56). Monn was not organist at Melk, and it seems that, if Albrechtsberger studied with him, it was before going to Melk in 1749.

33. Beethoven's exercises for Albrechtsberger still survive in great quantities (mainly in the Gesellschaft der Musikfreunde in Vienna). Many of them bear the tutor's corrections and improvements (see Nottebohm 1873).

34. Beethoven's knowledge of Latin, Italian, and French was quite extensive (he occasionally wrote letters in French), but his acquaintance with English remained extremely limited.

35. By the time Haydn returned, on 20 August 1795, Beethoven had probably completed his course with Albrechtsberger, and there is no evidence that he continued formal study with either of them after this date, although he maintained informal contacts and no doubt sought occasional advice from them.

36. The Elector Maximilian Franz had undoubtedly been generous to Beethoven but does not seem to have singled him out for any special favors in the way that some other patrons did. As Thayer points out, Beethoven never mentioned the Elector's generosity in any known correspondence and never dedicated a work to him (see Thayer, Forbes ed. 1967, 107).

37. Beethoven's salary from Bonn had been terminated in 1794, the same year that the Elector had ceased to rule there. Thus Beethoven was not entitled to expect a secure position there at any time after this. More-

over his family was no longer there by 1801:
his parents were dead, and his two surviving
brothers had followed him to Vienna.

38. This was the Lichnowsky family. Beethoven
lived at their home from about 1793 to
1795. Prince Lichnowsky also granted him
an annuity from 1800 until (probably) 1806.
Again Schlosser's dates are misleading.

39. The above passage is probably based mainly
on Gerber, who noted that in Beethoven's
early years in Vienna "he distinguished
himself even more as a virtuoso pianist"
than as a composer; Gerber continues:
"Everyone who had the chance to hear him
at this period (1800) agreed that he had at-
tained much greater speed and fire, although not always clarity. His forte, however, was free improvisation, and the art
of varying and developing a theme on
the spot—an art in which he resembled
Mozart" (Gerber, Wessely ed. 1966–77,
2:310).

40. Beethoven's music became widely appreciated in England during the first decade of
the nineteenth century. Several London
publishers applied to him, sometimes suc-
cessfully, for new works (see Tyson 1963),

and his music was often performed in concerts. More than once he was invited to England, although he does not appear to have been offered an actual position there.

41. Schlosser is probably referring here to Josephine Deym (née Brunsvik), whose husband had died in January 1804. Before long Beethoven was passionately in love with her, but by 1807 the relationship had cooled and he no doubt felt the great disappointment that Schlosser mentions.

42. Jerome Bonaparte (1784–1860) was the youngest brother of Napoleon and resided in Kassel during 1807–13 as "King of Westphalia." His offer to Beethoven was actually made in 1808, but the subsequent developments that Schlosser mentions took place the following year.

43. As stated in Gerber's lexicon, the initial agreement was for 4000 gulden or florins per annum (Gerber, Wessely ed. 1966–77, 2:315). The sum was made up of 1800 gulden from Prince Ferdinand Kinsky (1781–1812), 1500 from Archduke Rudolph (1788–1831; he was not yet Cardinal-Archbishop of Olmütz), and 700 from Prince Franz Joseph von Lobkowitz (1772–

1816). Inflation and devaluation soon reduced this to about 1600 gulden, but the three patrons raised their payments to a total of 3400 gulden (paper money), which was eventually worth 1360 gulden in silver. Thus Schlosser's reference to 2000 gulden corresponds to none of the actual figures and may simply be a misprint.

44. Beethoven's orchestral work *Wellington's Victory or The Battle of Vittoria* (Op. 91) was composed and first performed in 1813. During the Congress of Vienna in late 1814 it was performed three more times, before audiences that included several heads of state including Emperor Alexander I of Russia and his wife, Empress Elisabeth. Beethoven had some years earlier dedicated his Violin Sonatas, Op. 30, to the emperor, without receiving acknowledgment; he now presented his newly written Polonaise (Op. 89) to the empress and received 50 ducats for this and 100 for the sonatas (or, according to music historian Otto Jahn's account, double these amounts): see Thayer, Forbes ed. 1967, 603. Once again, Schlosser is approximately correct, but his figures are inexact.

45. Broadwood & Sons (London) sent Beethoven a new piano (dispatched 1817, arrived 1818) with the names of several leading London musicians inscribed, including the composers Ferdinand Ries, Frédéric Kalkbrenner, and Johann Baptist Cramer (Thayer, Forbes ed. 1967, 695). The instrument is now in the National Museum in Budapest.

46. Beethoven mentioned this honor in a letter to Franz Gerhard Wegeler on 7 December 1826 (Anderson 1961, 1322). He had been granted the Freedom of the City on 16 November 1815 (Thayer, Deiters and Riemann eds. 1917–23, 3:524).

47. Beethoven's deafness has been the subject of much speculation and controversy. It appears to have begun in about 1797 and gradually worsened, leading to the acute depression that is expressed in his Heiligenstadt Testament of 1802. He never became absolutely deaf, but from about 1818 his hearing was so weak that, as Schlosser mentions, people normally communicated with him in writing, using a slate or specially designated notebooks. The cause of his deafness, though it was certainly not that sug-

gested by Schlosser, has never been established. A recent theory that sarcoidosis was to blame (see Palferman 1992) is plausible but has not yet been confirmed.

48. These two sentences are expressly confirmed by Beethoven's friend Gerhard von Breuning, who quotes them in his book *Aus dem Schwarzspanierhause* (1874; see Breuning, Solomon ed. 1992, 44, 127).

49. The *Letters* of the 4th Earl of Chesterfield (1694–1773) were first published in 1774 and contain extensive advice on manners and conduct. Adolf von Knigge (1752–1796) published his *Über den Umgang mit Menschen* (On Social Intercourse) in 1788. Both books went through many editions during Beethoven's lifetime. Schlosser is not suggesting that Beethoven was not widely read but that he seemed unaware of all the niceties of polite manners.

50. Friedrich Wilhelm Rust (1739–1796) was a composer, violinist, and pianist from Dessau, where he was appointed court music director in 1775.

51. "Amphion [built] Thebes, I the house." The reference is to a story from Hesiod: he relates how Amphion (a singer, like Caf-

farelli) built the walls of Thebes in Greece, allegedly by moving the stones into place through the power of his music alone. (I am grateful to Susan Cooper for helping to elucidate this quotation.) Caffarelli's pompous attempt to liken himself to the legendary musician concurs well with the anecdote that Beethoven distributed.

52. Evidently one such copy of this lengthy tale had reached Schlosser, who could not resist publishing it complete.

53. This statement does not accord well with comments by other witnesses that Beethoven sometimes dressed inelegantly or relied on friends to replace his old clothes, and was once mistaken for a tramp. But some of these witnesses, such as Anton Schindler and Louis Schlösser, are unreliable, and it may be that Beethoven generally appeared smarter than we have been led to believe. At any rate, the picture presented here by Schlosser forms an interesting counterweight to other accounts.

54. This account of Beethoven's lodgings is broadly in line with others, but Schlosser greatly understates the sense of untidiness

that many of Beethoven's visitors experienced.

55. Considering the recognized greatness of Beethoven's art, this statement is extraordinary. Yet Schlosser was not the only writer with this opinion: Antonie Brentano (widely believed to have been Beethoven's "Immortal Beloved") wrote in 1819 that Beethoven was "as a human being greater than as an artist" (Solomon 1977, 182).

56. Beethoven's brothers Caspar Carl (1774–1815) and Nikolaus Johann (1776–1848) both moved to Vienna in the mid-1790s. Beethoven's relationship to Carl's son Karl (1806–1858) has been the subject of much controversy. For a balanced account, see Solomon 1977, 231–255.

57. Beethoven's principal illness at the end of his life was a liver disease, combined with dropsy; his heart remained strong. He was under constant medical supervision and treatment from early December until his death the following March—four months rather than six.

58. The Philharmonic Society of London resolved to send Beethoven 100 pounds on

28 February 1827, and Beethoven ac-
knowledged their gift with enormous gratitude on 18 March.

59. Stephan von Breuning (born 17 August
1774; died 4 June 1827) had known Beethoven since their childhood in Bonn.

60. The official record of Beethoven's estate
shows that he left only 1215 gulden in cash
(*Conventionsmünze*), plus 600 gulden in
Wiener Währung or paper money, which
was worth 240 gulden in *Conventionsmünze*.
This cash must have included the 100
pounds (about 1000 gulden) sent from
England. But he also left seven bank shares,
valued at 7441 gulden, and other property
(see Thayer, Forbes ed. 1967, 1072–1075).
It is unclear how Schlosser could have arrived at the figure he did.

61. Jacob Hotschevar, who became Karl's
guardian in June 1827 on the death of Breuning, published a notice on 20 September
1827 condemning Schlosser's book as
"filled with various significant inaccuracies"; he mentioned this passage in par-
ticular, stating that the funeral costs were
met from Beethoven's estate (Thayer, Deiters and Riemann eds. 1917–23, 5:500).

This is corroborated by the official record of Beethoven's estate, which notes that 650 gulden had been set aside "for funeral and other expenses" (Thayer, Forbes ed. 1967, 1072). The nephew's inheritance consisted primarily of the bank shares, which did remain untouched.

62. Franz Grillparzer (1791–1872) was a poet and playwright who had known Beethoven since about 1805. The two had begun to collaborate on an opera in the 1820s, but no musical sketches have been positively identified for it. Heinrich Anschütz (1785–1865) was also acquainted with Beethoven.

63. At least three versions of Grillparzer's funeral oration are known, and it is impossible at this distance to be sure which precise words were spoken by Anschütz. Grillparzer himself delivered one version to Stephan von Breuning, whose son Gerhard copied it "then and there" and later published it in his book *Aus dem Schwarzspanierhause* (1874; see Breuning, Solomon ed. 1992, 109); this version is also published in Thayer, Deiters and Riemann eds. 1917–1923, 5:496–497. The version published in Grillparzer's *Collected Works* has

been reprinted in Nettl 1958, 136–137, and translated in Sonneck 1967, 229–231, and Thayer, Forbes ed. 1967, 1057–1058, as well as in Breuning, Solomon ed. 1992, 109–110. In the latter, Solomon also notes all the variants in Breuning's version. Schlosser's version derives from that printed in "several journals"; it seems to lie somewhere between the other two, apart from a few odd places where the Schlosser text may easily have been corrupted. This suggests that Breuning may have had access to an early version, which was revised before appearing in the newspapers and Schlosser, and was touched up again by Grillparzer before the *Collected Works* version. The main differences lie in Schlosser's final two paragraphs, where all three versions diverge. Breuning's reads thus:

> You, however, who have followed our funeral procession thus far, overcome your mourning. For it is not a depressing but an uplifting feeling to stand at the coffin of the man of whom one may say, as of no one else: he has achieved great things, and was beyond reproach. Go from here

lamenting, but composed. Take with you—a flower from his grave—in memory of him and his works. And if ever the force of his creations overwhelms you like an onrushing tempest, then recall the memory of today, the memory of him, who achieved such great things and who was beyond reproach.

The *Collected Works* version reads thus:

You, however, who have followed our funeral train thus far, overcome your grief. You have not lost him, you have won him. No living man enters the halls of the immortals. Not until the body has perished, do their portals open. He whom you mourn stands from now onward among the great of all ages, inviolate forever. Return homeward, therefore, sorrowful but composed.And if ever the force of his creations overwhelms you like an onrushing tempest, when your ecstasy overflows amid a generation as yet unborn, then remember this hour and think: we were there when they buried him, and when he died, we wept.

64. Cherubini's Requiem in C minor, which Beethoven is said to have particularly admired, dates from 1816 (his second Requiem, for men's voices, dates from 1836).

65. Ignaz Schuppanzigh (1776–1830) was a noted violinist and friend of Beethoven.

66. The Fourth Symphony (Op. 60) and the overture to *The Consecration of the House* (Op. 124).

67. Franz Xaver Gebauer (1784–1822) established the Concerts Spirituels in Vienna in 1819, borrowing the name from the series in Paris. Ferdinand Piringer (1780–1829) was initially Gebauer's assistant and became a close friend of Beethoven during the 1820s.

68. All the music was well known but relatively early, the most recent being the Fifth Symphony of 1807–08 and the earliest being the song *Adelaide* (Op. 46), published in 1797. Seidl's poem is in Breuning 1907, 175 (translated in Breuning, Solomon ed. 1992, 110–111).

69. Beethoven sat for Dietrich in 1819–20, and the sculptor also made use of Beethoven's life mask produced by Franz Klein in 1812. Dietrich then made several copies of the

bust, some of them dated 1821 (see Landon 1970, 15).

70. August Friedrich Kanne (1778–1833) was a composer and poet, and a friend of Beethoven.

71. Ignaz Franz Castelli (1781–1862) was an acquaintance of Beethoven and was present at the funeral, where a poem of his was distributed. Anton Diabelli (1781–1858) was a publisher in Vienna and composer of the waltz on which Beethoven wrote his Variations Op. 120. Joseph Drechsler (1782–1852), who also wrote a variation on Diabelli's waltz, was a prolific composer, for whom Beethoven wrote a recommendation in 1823 (Anderson 1961, 1070).

72. The date of this occasion is noteworthy, since Schlosser's preface is dated June 1827 and his book was in print by September. Vincenz Mašek (1755–1831) was a prolific composer and prominent music director in Prague.

73. Ignaz Seyfried (1776–1841) was a composer and close acquaintance of Beethoven for many years. Joseph Schubert (1757–1837) was a German violinist unrelated to Franz Schubert. Albin Mašek (1804–

1878), son of Vincenz, was like his father a composer and music director in Prague. The Miserere was an adaptation for four-part men's chorus of the first of Beethoven's three Equali for four trombones (WoO 30); these had been composed in Linz in 1812 for Franz Glöggl. This piece was eminently suitable for the occasion Schlosser describes, since the equali had been composed as funeral music (see Kinsky 1955, 470). The event was also described in similar terms in a report in the *Monatschrift der Gesellschaft des Vaterländischen Museums* (September 1827, 85); see Pulkert 1988, 427.

74. No copy of such a list is known.

75. Many of Beethoven's opus numbers are in chronological order, but there are plenty of exceptions, such as the piano sonatas of Opus 49, and *King Stephen*, Op. 117.

76. Op. 1 (1795). These trios were not, of course, Beethoven's first composition or publication.

77. Schlosser presumably means Beethoven's Septet, Op. 20, of 1799, although Beethoven did write two sextets, Op. 71 and Op. 81b, during this period. The other works

mentioned—his first two symphonies and his first six quartets—all date from a brief time span, 1798–1802.

78. The works between Opus 40 and Opus 60 include a number that had been held over from earlier, but the main ones date from the period 1801–06. The *Eroica*, Op. 55, dates from 1803–04.

79. Schlosser, like most writers since, divides Beethoven's creative output into three periods, but places the onset of the third much earlier than normal, with the Fifth Symphony of 1807–08.

80. It was already becoming fashionable to consider Beethoven's vocal music inferior to his instrumental, but Schlosser's criticism here seems misplaced. That Beethoven paid great attention to both the meaning and the rhythm of the words is amply attested in many works, as well as in his sketches (see Cooper 1990, 219–241). His concern for good verbal rhythm is also illustrated in his letter to Stadler that Schlosser reproduced, where Beethoven's criticism appears to be directed at this aspect of the music he quotes.

81. Early performances of *Fidelio* in 1805–06 were by all accounts poor in quality and were indeed unsuccessful. Even after its revival in 1814 it was found extremely difficult to perform, but it soon enjoyed increasing success.

82. Johann Friedrich Reichardt (1752–1814) was a composer and writer on music who visited Vienna in 1808–09; the following year he published his *Vertraute Briefe* describing his visit (modern edition, ed. Gustav Gugitz, Munich, 1915). Precisely the same extract from Reichardt is quoted in Gerber's lexicon (Gerber, Wessely ed. 1966–77, 2:316), which was presumably Schlosser's source.

83. This comparison to Shakespeare is remarkable, but Beethoven had already been compared to him by certain other observers such as George Thomson and Amadeus Wendt.

84. The title of Schiller's poem is *Die Macht des Gesanges* (The Power of Song). Schlosser quotes the first of five stanzas, changing only Schiller's ninth line, which reads, "So strömen des Gesanges Wellen." (Dr. Pauly

and I are indebted to Professor Laureen Nussbaum for the identification.)

85. Nothing from this ambitious list of supplementary material is known to have appeared.

86. The first passage Beethoven quotes is from bar 34 of the Kyrie in Mozart's Requiem, but Mozart did not write the lower quarter notes, which would create a rather muddy texture and obscure the sixteenth-note bass line. In the second and third passages, evidently from a mass by Gottfried Weber, Beethoven is apparently objecting to the word setting, which certainly distorts the natural verbal rhythm. In the Mozart extract, Beethoven's crosses apply to the bass quarter notes, but in the Weber ones, it is the notes between the two crosses in each pair that are faulty. (Most transcriptions of this letter omit or misplace some of Beethoven's crosses.)

87. The references are to Johann Franz Xaver Sterkel (1750–1817); Wolfgang Nicolaus Haueisen (1740–1804); Christian Kalkbrenner (1763–1806), father of the more famous Frédéric Kalkbrenner (1785–1849);

and Johann André (1741–1799). Beethoven makes a pun out of the last name, since
"andre" means "other": the "other" André
is the son Johann Anton (1775–1842). Beethoven is evidently suggesting that Weber's
music is not merely clumsy but very old-
fashioned.

88. Beethoven had regarded Mozart as the
greatest of all composers, until he came to
know the music of Handel, whom he then
regarded more highly.

References

Albrecht, Theodore, and Elaine Schwensen. 1988. "More than just *Peanuts*: Evidence for December 16 as Beethoven's Birthday." *The Beethoven Newsletter* 3:51, 60–63.

Anderson, Emily, trans. and ed. 1961. *The Letters of Beethoven*. 3 vols. London: Macmillan Press Ltd.

Brenneis, Clemens. 1979. "Das Fischhof-Manuskript: Zur Frühgeschichte der Beethoven-Biographik." In *Zu Beethoven: Aufsätze und Annotationen*. Ed. Harry Goldschmidt. Berlin: Verlag Neue Musik. 90–116.

Breuning, Gerhard von. Ed. Maynard Solomon. 1992. *Memories of Beethoven*. Trans. Henry Mins and Maynard Solomon (from *Aus dem Schwarzspanierhause*, 1874, 2nd ed., 1907). Cambridge, England: Cambridge University Press.

Cooper, Barry. 1990. *Beethoven and the Creative Process*. Oxford: Clarendon Press.

Gärtner, Heinz. 1991. *Constanze Mozart: After the Requiem*. Trans. Reinhard G. Pauly. Portland: Amadeus Press.

Gerber, Ernst Ludwig. Ed. Othmar Wessely. 1966–77. *Historisch-biographisches Lexikon der Tonkünstler; Neues historisch-biographisches Lexikon der Tonkünstler; Ergänzungen—Berichtigungen—Nachträge.* 4 vols. Graz: Akademische Druck- und Verlagsanstalt.

Kinsky, Georg. Ed. and completed by Hans Halm. 1955. *Das Werk Beethovens: Thematisch-bibliographisches Verzeichnis seiner sämtlichen vollendeten Kompositionen.* Munich: Henle.

Landon, H. C. Robbins. 1970. *Beethoven: A Documentary Study.* London: Thames & Hudson.

——. 1976. *Haydn: Chronicle and Works.* Vol. 3, *Haydn in England 1791–1795.* London: Thames & Hudson.

Letters to the editor. 1994. "Picturing Beethoven." *Journal of the American Musicological Society* 47:178–190.

Nettl, Paul. 1958. *Beethoven.* Frankfurt: Fischer.

Nottebohm, Gustav. 1873. *Beethoven's Studien.* Leipzig and Winterthur: Rieter-Biedermann.

Palferman, Thomas. 1992. "Beethoven's Medical History: Themes and Variations." *The Beethoven Newsletter* 7:2–9.

Pečman, Rudolf. 1978. "Mozart oder Beethoven? Eine Grundfrage des Prager Musikmilieus der ersten Dezennien des 19. Jahrhunderts." In *Bericht über den Internationalen Beethoven-Kongress Berlin 1977*. Ed. Harry Goldschmidt and others. Leipzig: VEB Deutscher Verlag für Musik. 345–350.

Pulkert, Oldřich. 1988. "Die zeitgenössische Beethoven-Rezeption in den böhmischen Ländern." In *Beethoven und Böhmen*. Ed. Sieghard Brandenburg and Martella Gutiérrez-Denhoff. Bonn: Beethoven-Haus. 409–433.

Schlosser, Johann Aloys. Ed. Oldřich Pulkert. 1993. *Wolfgang Amad. Mozart. Eine begründete und ausführliche Biographie desselben*. Prague: Editio Resonus.

Solomon, Maynard. 1977. *Beethoven*. New York: Schirmer Books.

——. 1988. *Beethoven Essays*. Cambridge, Mass.: Harvard University Press.

Sonneck, Oscar G., ed. 1967. *Beethoven: Impressions by His Contemporaries*. New York: Dover Publications. Originally published 1926.

Steblin, Rita. 1992. "The Newly Discovered Hochenecker Portrait of Beethoven (1819):

'Das ähnlichste Bildnis Beethovens.'" *Journal of the American Musicological Society* 45: 468–497.

Thayer, Alexander Wheelock. Ed. and completed by Hermann Deiters and Hugo Riemann. 1917–23. *Ludwig van Beethovens Leben*. 5 vols. Leipzig: Breitkopf & Härtel.

——. Revised and ed. Elliot Forbes. 1967. *Thayer's Life of Beethoven*. 2nd ed. Princeton, N.J.: Princeton University Press.

Tyson, Alan. 1963. *The Authentic English Editions of Beethoven*. London: Faber.

Wegeler, Franz, and Ferdinand Ries. 1987. *Remembering Beethoven*. Trans. Frederick Noonan (from *Biographische Notizen über Ludwig van Beethoven*, 1838 and 1845). Introduction by Eva Badura-Skoda. Arlington, Va.: Great Ocean Publishers.

Index

Mozart zu schreiben will,

musste ... ... *Meisterwerk*

... ...

— gnus dei

pec- ca- — ta mundi

qui tollis peccata qui

tollis peccata

... ...

... ...

requiescant in pace —